Learning for Life

Learning for Life

An Imaginative Approach
to Worldview Education
in the Context of Diversity

ANDRÉ MULDER
&
BAS VAN DEN BERG

WIPF & STOCK · Eugene, Oregon

LEARNING FOR LIFE
An Imaginative Approach to Worldview Education in the Context of Diversity

Copyright © 2019 André Mulder and Bas van den Berg. All rights reserved. Except for brief quotations in critical publications or reviews, no part of this book may be reproduced in any manner without prior written permission from the publisher. Write: Permissions, Wipf and Stock Publishers, 199 W. 8th Ave., Suite 3, Eugene, OR 97401.

Wipf & Stock
An Imprint of Wipf and Stock Publishers
199 W. 8th Ave., Suite 3
Eugene, OR 97401

www.wipfandstock.com

PAPERBACK ISBN: 978-1-5326-7686-4
HARDCOVER ISBN: 978-1-5326-7687-1
EBOOK ISBN: 978-1-5326-7688-8

Manufactured in the U.S.A.   FEBRUARY 18, 2019

This work was supported by Sia RAAK Publiek, grant number 2014-01-38P

Contents

Introduction On Track with Learning for Life | vii

Chapter 1 European Challenges for Worldview Education | 1
    1.1. Position of Worldview Education in Public and in Private Schools | 1
    1.2. Worldview Education and Policies of the European Union | 7
    1.3. Reference Book, Toledo Guidelines, and Signposts | 10
    1.4. Hermeneutical Approach in Europe and the Challenge of Hermeneutical Juggling | 12

Chapter 2 The Dutch Challenge: Developments in Worldview Education | 17
    2.1. Post-pillarized Education in a Secularized and Pluralized Context | 17
    2.2. Current practices in Dutch Worldview Education: Two Primary Schools | 23
    2.3. An Empowering Learning Environment for Worldview Education | 27

Chapter 3 Learning for Life: A Hermeneutical-Communicative Model for Worldview Education | 37
    3.1. Hermeneutical-Communicative Learning | 37
    3.2. The Hermeneutical-Communicative Model | 41

Chapter 4 Staging Dialogical Worldview Education: Research Outcomes | 58

4.1. Practice Development and Research | 58
4.2. Portraits of Nine Learning for Life schools | 61
4.3. Data, Meta-Analysis, and Results from Learning for Life | 93
4.4. The Model: Did it Work? | 109

Chapter 5 Requirements for Teachers and Teams to Meet the Challenge | 112

5.1. Three Fields of Tension in the Transition from Transfer-Oriented toward Student-Oriented Worldview Education | 113
5.2. Roles and Competencies of Teachers | 123

Reflection The Road Ahead | 130

A Promising Model | 131
A Vulnerable Model | 133
The Road Ahead | 135

Appendix A Toledo Learning Outcomes | 137

Appendix B Toledo Key Principles for Teaching Worldview Education | 139

Appendix C List of Participants | 143

Project Manager | 143
Participating Schools | 143
Participating Universities | 143
Participating Researchers | 144

Bibliography | 145

Introduction

On Track with Learning for Life

SINCE THE 1960S, TURBULENT changes have emerged in the religious landscape of the Netherlands. Secularization, individualization, migration, and pluralization drive these changes toward religious diversity, leading to increased atheism and agnosticism. These changes hugely affected religious institutions like churches, schools, hospitals, trade unions, sports clubs, civic associations, and welfare organizations. They saw a gradual and sometimes even rapid change in their constituent membership. A more or less uniform religious orientation within these populations, with accompanying rituals and ethical practices, was dissolving into a mixture of personalized, individualistic, and hybrid worldview constructions, no longer resembling one single tradition. Moreover, institutions had to reflect on continuity due to a rapid decline in members, and they had to reflect on identity due to the shift in religious composition of the religious worldview of their members or participants.

Schools and teaching teams did not remain unaffected by these changes. In private schools (most of which are religious schools in the Netherlands), more and more teachers no longer fully identified with the religious roots and the identity of the school. The individualization in religious identity construction did not stop at the door of religious institutions themselves. The result is internal pluralization in convictions and ethical and spiritual

Introduction

practices. In addition, the majority of students at most of the religious schools no longer belong to a church or to the tradition in which the religious schools are rooted.

The changing context of the school together with the internal changes in population triggered reflection and innovation in religious education, reaching full momentum in the 1980s and still continuing today. The question of how to address the universal human search for meaning in an educational context is topical and pressing. In the past decade, we have seen an awareness in public schools of the importance of worldview education in public schools, which by law should be "neutral" regarding life philosophy and religion. Teaching teams and school classes represent the full range of diversity in worldview orientation, and the debates about the role of religion in the public realm (e.g., building mosques, wearing headscarves or crosses) cannot be kept outside the school. A growing number of public schools feel the need to reflect on the subject of worldview education to prepare children for democratic citizenship in a highly diverse society. So, we see two school types—public schools and private schools—both searching for modern ways to address questions of meaning in life, the role of traditions, and the function of rituals. There is an urge to innovate.

We use the term *worldview education* to refer to educational practices aimed at developing a worldview identity in the school context. A worldview is a more or less coherent view of life, humanity, and the world that makes exploration of answers to existential questions possible, contains moral values, provides meaning in people's lives, and aims to influence their thinking and acting.[1] Many teachers, especially in private schools (generally religious schools), are used to the concept of religious education. The concept of worldview education, however, has considerable advantages. First of all, worldview comprises religious and nonreligious views of life.[2] This means that it suits both public and private schools. Second, it considers multiple sources for meaning, which is useful in understanding how modern people combine religious

1. Kooij, *Worldview and Moral Education*, 35.
2. Mulder, *Introductie: Werken met Diepgang*.

Introduction

and nonreligious sources in their patchwork worldview identity. In other words, a broader definition acknowledges intrapersonal diversity and hybrid identities. And third, a worldview approach includes the ability to discern between organizational and personal constructs and makes it easier to learn about and from religion.[3]

It is our strong conviction that there is no one single answer to the question of developing modern forms of worldview education that are appropriate to the context of public and private schools, and that the answers can only be found when scholars, teachers, and principals work together. Acknowledging the unique and contextually constructed identity of every school, while respecting the intra-school and the inter-school diversity in the two school types, we initiated a search for a model for reflection on worldview education that addresses general perspectives drawn from religious pedagogy and didactics.

Over the last seven years, this journey has taken place in different action research projects in primary schools of both types. Our efforts culminated in our most recent government-funded project: Learning for Life.

This book reports on the project in the context of developments in religion and education in Europe (chapter 1) and in the Netherlands (chapter 2). Our Learning for Life project shows that it is possible to innovate worldview education by choosing a radical focus on the development of the students' worldview identity. Using the hermeneutical-communicative model for worldview education, the teacher can create a dynamic and powerful dialogical learning environment that contributes to the worldview development of every student, regardless of the religious or nonreligious orientation of the student or the teacher. Within our model, every school team can contextualize and mold their worldview education in such a way that it fits the specific characteristics of their cultural and religious identity. The model is hermeneutical, oriented toward construction of meaning from religious and nonreligious sources related to existential questions; the model is communicative, aimed at a dialogue-style exchange of experiences and

3. Kooij, *Worldview and Moral Education*, 58.

Introduction

convictions between students and between students and teacher (chapter 3). We implemented the model in the specific contexts in nine schools, which were as diverse as the Dutch educational landscape can be (chapter 4). We monitored the process and the findings during this two-year project; on that basis, we present some major observations. We established that the appropriation of this model is not an easy road. Existing practices and teaching attitudes have been shaped over a long period of time. They need significant changes to work toward the three educational aims of the model: clarification of existence; handling diversity; and worldview literacy. Teachers need some specific competencies to work within the framework of the model fruitfully (chapter 5).

We are convinced that our model can be useful in all kinds of contexts when major shifts in attitude toward organizational religion take place, and major changes in the composition of student bodies.[4] The model honors the wisdom from religious and non-religious sources, fosters dialogue in a culturally and religiously diverse society, contributes to the students' process of searching for meaning, specifically with regard to existential questions, and provides opportunities for teachers and students to share what is of utmost importance to them in a pedagogical safe space.

---

4. A list of participants in the project Learning for Life can be found in appendix C.

Chapter 1
European Challenges for Worldview Education

LEARNING FOR LIFE IS a project that shares its characteristics with the culture and society in which it was designed and executed; it is a Dutch affair. We shall explore the Dutch educational system and laws in the next chapter. However, as a Dutch project, it could not have become what it was without the influence of the wider context of Europe. Although every country has its own political and religious history in Europe, our project bears the traces of culture and religious climate of the surrounding countries. In this chapter, we share some features of this European context that are relevant to the understanding of *Learning for Life*. We focus on the educational system and the position of worldview education in public and private schools, as well on the collective policy on education and religion within the European Union. We close this chapter with a hermeneutical approach to worldview education which is applied across Europe.

1.1. POSITION OF WORLDVIEW EDUCATION IN PUBLIC AND IN PRIVATE SCHOOLS

Over the past decades, the position of worldview education at religious and public schools as well as its goals and content have been discussed throughout the countries of Europe, at national levels as well as at a European level. Two reasons can be found for this debate: the first is the secularization process that affects all European countries, although not all in the same way and with the same intensity. By secularization, we mean the changes in religious belonging and in religious believing. People tend to give meaning to their lives less in correspondence with the traditional churches, their practices, and beliefs. This raises the question of the structural position of religious schools, the freedom to start religious schools and state funding of religious schools. All of them have been given form in the sociocultural, religious, and political situation of the past, which has changed significantly in recent years. One may ask whether the position of religious schools still reflects the current religious practice of the majority of the inhabitants of many European countries. Some speak of a "mismatch."[1] This mismatch can consist of a dominance of private schools in a predominantly secularized society or of a strong influence or a privileged position of the church regarding the content of worldview education in a society with low numbers of church affiliation. Looking at the Netherlands, we learn from the European Values Study (1981–2008) that the Netherlands is among the most secularized European countries, looking at variables like "belief in God" or "belief in sin," church affiliation and religious practices.[2]

The second reason for the debate about position and content of worldview education is 9/11 and the subsequent discussions about Islam and its position in countries stemming from a Christian tradition and hallmarked by Christian values. And we add that not only the number of adherents to Islam is growing in several European countries, but also the number of different religious groups. Pluralization of religion is increasing. The ongoing questions therefore are how Europe can create safe and stable societies in which there is room for different religious and non-religious belief systems and what roles education in general and worldview education in particular must play to prepare children

1. Smith et al., introduction to *Worldview Education*, 1.
2. Van den Brink, *De Lage Landen en het Hogere*, 93, 130, 136, 241.

European Challenges for Worldview Education

for a peaceful multicultural and multireligious society. Handling religious diversity seems to be a long-lasting challenge for schools and governments.

In answering these questions, we must differentiate between *public* and *private* (most of the time *religious*) schools. The subject of worldview education is approached differently within these two educational varieties. The position of religious schools, often started by churches, differs enormously in the European countries, due to historical developments, the power of churches, and the outcome of church/state debates in the eighteenth and nineteenth centuries. Some important indicators are:[3]

- the relationship between church and state, e.g., whether or not there is a national or official religion;
- the teaching of religion in public schools (compulsory, optional, or absent) and the content and aim of the subject (e.g., faith identity formation or information about world religions);
- the subsidization of private schools by the state, the scope of state contributions, and the regulations connected to it;
- the existence of a common national curriculum;
- freedom of staff policy in private schools;
- state control of quality of education.

One common denominator is that all countries in Europe allow the establishment of private schools. There are substantial differences between the other characteristics. All countries except France have some form of worldview education in public (state-provided) schools, although this subject is not compulsory in all countries. Sometimes students can opt out (e.g., United Kingdom, Austria, Belgium) or have to opt in (e.g., Estonia, Czech Republic, Hungary, the Netherlands).

The countries also differ in what laws oblige to be offered as content in worldview education. This content differs from

---

3. Avram and Dronkers, "Religion and Schooling," 22–28.

so-called "objective" information about major religions present in the specific countries or content about the religion or church of the choice of the parents or student. At private schools, worldview education is compulsory for all students. The governments of the European countries have no direct influence on the content of worldview education provided at private schools. Indirectly, they may have some influence through state quality control systems and requirements for staffing.

Concerning state funding of church or faith schools, Avram and Dronkers identify four types:[4]

- *integrated educational systems* with equal funding (e.g., Denmark, Spain, the Netherlands);
- *denominative supportive educational systems* in which some denominations receive more funding, sometimes a lot more, than other private schools (e.g., Austria, Portugal, United Kingdom);
- *eclectic educational system* with varying degrees of funding, but always less than the amount provided to public schools (e.g., Belgium, Germany, Italy);
- *segregated educational system* with no funding for private schools at all (e.g., Greece, Bulgaria, Romania).

The last category only exists in Eastern Orthodox countries where the church has a massive influence on state schools and on state-regulated worldview education in these schools.

To illustrate the differences between the European countries, we present the situation in our neighboring countries: Germany and Belgium.

---

4. Avram and Dronkers, "Religion and Schooling," 25.

European Challenges for Worldview Education

Germany

In Germany, religious pluralization and individualization of religious and nonreligious worldviews is strongly recognizable.[5] Generally, 30% of the population belongs to the Roman Catholic Church and 30% to the Evangelical Church, 5% are Muslims, and 1.9% belongs to Orthodox Churches. About 34% are not affiliated with a religion. This general picture can differ moderately when northern parts of the country are compared with southern or western parts. The picture can differ strongly when compared to the eastern part of Germany or to the bigger cities. Eighty percent of the population in former East Germany state non-affiliation with religion. Hamburg, for instance, has 106 different religious groups, including 10% belonging to the Roman Catholic Church. Germany has a moderate separation of church and state. Church taxes are collected by the state, and the constitution refers to God and prescribes worldview education in state schools. However, students and teachers have freedom to participate in worldview education. The state provides funding for the subject, while religious groups are responsible for the content. In most of the German federal states, worldview education has a curriculum containing information about convictions, rituals, and history of a specific denomination (most of the time Roman Catholic or Protestant). Churches are allowed to cooperate in an ecumenical curriculum. Some federal states, which are by law in control of education within the borders of the state, made worldview education optional (sometimes together with humanistic social studies). Some kept worldview education optional but introduced a compulsory subject of ethics/values. In Germany, the number of church-related schools in the private sector is increasing. Worldview education at these schools is focused on religious socialization. In Protestant worldview education, the competence to participate in a pluralistic society with a solid personal religious identity has received more attention in recent years. In Roman Catholic education, the attention seems to be directed more and more toward catechism, in a

---

5. Rothgangel et al., *Worldview Education at Schools in Germany*, 115ff.

societal environment in which more and more children grow up religiously illiterate.

Belgium

In the federal state of Belgium, religious diversity is increasing.[6] Although it was historically a Catholic country, church affiliation has been dropping dramatically in the last decades. Nowadays, about 50% of the Belgians belong to the Roman Catholic Church, and 43% declare themselves nonreligious or atheists; 7% adhere to another religion, and the number of Muslims is increasing. The figures vary in the different parts of Belgium, which can be illustrated by the percentage of students taking religious classes: in Flanders, 82% of the children in secondary schools participate in Roman Catholic worldview education and 5% Islamic lessons; in Brussels, 43% attend Islamic lessons and 15.2% attend Roman Catholic classes; in Wallonia, 26.4% register for Roman Catholic classes, 7.8% for Islamic classes, and the majority of 64.2% attends the nonreligious classes about morality. Most private schools are Catholic. The constitution of Belgium protects freedom of religion, which implies equal treatment of the recognized religions. The state supports a plurality of worldviews. Therefore, public schools are compelled to offer worldview education in all six recognized religions present in Belgium and in Freemasonry. Private schools can choose any type of worldview education to offer. Most of the private schools are Catholic and are linked with a diocese or congregation. And most of the students attend private schools, so at least 60% of all students in Belgium receive Catholic worldview education.

The pluralization of religion together with the decline in church affiliation prompted the debate about the content of Catholic worldview education. This debate takes place within the schools themselves. A movement in the direction of dialogical education (instead of a monological introduction to the Catholic

---

6. Derroitte et al., *Worldview Education*, 43ff.

faith) is visible. A threefold task is incorporated in such a dialogical approach: sensitizing students to the plurality of worldviews in the society; confronting students with the Christian (including Catholic) religion in the context of this plurality; enabling students to develop their own religious identity in dialogue with the Christian religion. The debate on aims and didactics in worldview education in Catholic schools in Belgium is strongly influenced by the development of a hermeneutical-communicative approach by Lombaerts, Maex, and Pollefeyt.[7]

1.2. WORLDVIEW EDUCATION AND POLICIES OF THE EUROPEAN UNION

Far from seeing it as a private matter, the Organization for Security and Co-operation in Europe (OSCE) values religion as an important topic in public education. It is clear that there is not now, nor has there been a monoculture in Europe. In its *Toledo Guiding Principles on Teaching about Religion and Beliefs in Public Schools* (*Toledo*), the OSCE states: "Modern-day Europe is the result of the interweaving of migrations of disparate peoples, interactions of religions within a cradle molded by Christianity and by other religious and cultural forces for more than twenty-five centuries, through borrowing, copying, transforming, transmitting, and absorbing."[8] High-quality education on religion and beliefs should be implemented at all public schools grounded on two principles: "First, that there is positive value in teaching that emphasizes respect for everyone's right to freedom of religion and belief, and second, that teaching about religions and beliefs can reduce harmful misunderstandings and stereotypes."[9] The OSCE is convinced that sound worldview education contributes to tolerance and nondiscrimination, fosters social integration and democratic

---

7. Lombaerts, *Hermeneutical-Communicative Concept*; Maex, *Een Hermeneutisch-Communicatief Concept*; Pollefeyt, *Difference Matters*; *Difference of Alterity*; *Reader Course Didactics*.
8. OSCE/ODIHR, *Toledo Guiding Principles*, Introduction.
9. OSCE/ODIHR, *Toledo Guiding Principles*, 12.

citizenship. These positive outcomes of worldview education can only be reached when freedom of thought, consciousness and religion is respected.

The OSCE accounts for four reasons to teach about religions and beliefs:

- Religions and beliefs are important forces in the lives of individuals and communities and therefore have great significance for society as a whole. Understanding these convictions is necessary if people are to understand one another in our diverse societies, and also if they are to appreciate the significance of the rights that protect them.

- Learning about religions and beliefs contributes to forming and developing self-understanding, including a deeper appreciation of one's own religion or belief. Studying about religions and beliefs opens students' minds to questions of meaning and purpose and exposes students to critical ethical issues addressed by humankind throughout history.

- Much history, literature and culture is unintelligible without knowledge of religions and beliefs. Therefore, study about religions and beliefs is an essential part of an all-round education. Learning about religions and beliefs forms part of one's own stock of education, broadens one's horizon and deepens one's insight into the complexities of both past and present.

- Knowledge of religions and beliefs can help promote respectful behavior and enhance social cohesion. In this sense, all members of society, irrespective of their own convictions, benefit from knowledge about the religious and belief systems of others.[10]

Toledo is an instruction for teaching *about* religion, although it does not prefer this approach for worldview education and acknowledges that there are other possibly fruitful approaches that leave room for the protection of human rights, like teaching *into* religion or teaching *from* religion. The principles and suggestions

10. OSCE/ODIHR, *Toledo Guiding Principles*, 19.

of *Toledo* are also applicable in religious or nonreligious private schools with courses about religions and worldviews. *Toledo* assists governments in the construction of curricula, teacher education, pedagogy, and cooperation within the framework of human rights. *Toledo* is in line with the Council of Europe (CoE) *Recommendation on Education and Religion* (2005), which holds that all member states are encouraged to provide worldview education in primary and secondary public schools.[11] The recommendation states that democratic citizenship requires knowledge of religions and an attitude of tolerance. As this knowledge is dying out in families during upbringing, schools should take responsibility for teaching students about religion and worldviews. The recommendation sees schools as a major force in combating stereotypes, misunderstanding, and ignorance of religion and in fostering critical spirits and tolerance. According to the CoE, countries do not invest enough in realizing these goals. This recommendation was followed by *Recommendation 12* (2008) of the committee of Ministers of Education, saying: "Pursue initiatives in the field of intercultural education relating to the diversity of religions and nonreligious convictions in order to promote tolerance and the development of a culture of 'living together.'" The "Intercultural Education and the Challenge of Religious Diversity and Dialogue in Europe" project was an outcome of the 2005 recommendation; this project resulted in a reference book for schools on religious diversity and intercultural education.[12] In 2014, the council also released a document with a perspective on teaching about religions and nonreligious worldviews in intercultural education, entitled *Signposts*. All these statements and products aim at respectful and tolerant European societies in which freedom of religion and freedom of speech are protected and in which its members have a sound knowledge of religious and nonreligious worldviews in order to be able to handle differences and live peacefully.

---

11. CoE, *Recommendation 1720*
12. CoE, *Religious Diversity and Intercultural Education*.

Learning for Life

1.3. REFERENCE BOOK, TOLEDO GUIDELINES, AND SIGNPOSTS

The products of the European Union with regard to worldview education cannot be described in full length in this book. We present the highlights which inspired us in our *Learning for Life* project.

The *Reference Book* is a source for reflection and application of educational forms and tools with regard to the religious dimension of intercultural education. It addresses theoretical perspectives, educational considerations, educational policy, and examples from practice (good practices) with respect to religious diversity in education. Religion is seen as a cultural phenomenon, mostly but not exclusively residing in the private realm of human life, but nevertheless underlying and motivating social action. Because of the enormous diversity in Europe, it is important to prepare children to have understanding in religion, while this diversity is manifest in schools. Values in the religious dimension in intercultural education are: tolerance, reciprocity, civic-mindedness. The *Reference Book* not only has a helpful glossary explaining keywords like diversity, religion, and so on, but also a superb chapter by Robert Jackson about religion and religious diversity, making distinctions between pluralism and plurality, ethnicity and religiosity, multiculturality and interculturality, and so forth.

The section on methodology considers four conditions for fruitful intercultural education: cooperative learning; a safe space to foster self-expression; using "distancing" and "simulation"; empathetic communication. Within these conditions, four possible approaches are discussed and illustrated: a phenomenological approach, an interpretive approach, a dialogical approach, and a contextual approach. Our *Learning for Life* project combines the interpretive with the dialogical approach. The *Reference Book* ends with a bunch of inspiring examples from Cyprus, Norway, Greece, France, United Kingdom, Italy, Slovenia, Spain, and Austria. The examples stretch from single lessons to complete festivals and educational weeks.

European Challenges for Worldview Education

The *Toledo Guidelines* were already referenced above. They offer practical principles, procedures, and standards for preparing curricula about religions and beliefs (the latter interpreted as non-religious worldviews). Again, a human rights perspective is taken, consistent with European policy since the establishment of the European Union: "Teaching about religions and beliefs should be sensitive, balanced, inclusive, nondoctrinal, impartial, and based on human rights principles relating to freedom of religion or belief. This implies that considerations relating to the freedom of religion or belief should pervade any curricula developed for teaching about religions and beliefs."[13] *Toledo* presents a comprehensive list of learning outcomes for worldview education (see appendix A: "*Toledo* Learning Outcomes"). These outcomes include knowledge about worldview and human rights, development of values and of a critical attitude. The outcomes are relevant to every form of worldview education in every national and cultural context, be it provided in a public or private school. A summary of the key guiding principles for teaching worldview education is presented in appendix B. These principles show great sensitivity for the contextual, contemporary, and historical aspects of religion, and value sound scientific information, the fostering of religious freedom, and the professionality of worldview teachers.

Seven years after *Toledo* and as a result of Recommendation 12 (2008), Robert Jackson wrote *Signposts* on behalf of the Council of Europe to help the member countries to implement dimensions of religious and non-religious convictions in intercultural education. *Signposts* understands learning about religion as a comprehensive way of learning:

> In relation to religions, it is not sufficient to teach about the history of religions, or about the outward phenomena of religions. Religion is not restricted to practices, artefacts and buildings. It is also necessary to attempt to understand the meaning of religious language as used by religious believers, including expressions of their beliefs, values and emotions. Such understanding requires

13. OSCE/ODIHR, *Toledo*, 40.

Learning for Life

knowledge, but it also requires certain attitudes and skills that raise self-awareness and awareness and understanding of the beliefs and values of others, as well as values affirming human dignity.[14]

We adopted this view for our *Learning for Life* project.

Signposts addresses the following topics: terminology; competence, and didactics; the classroom as a "safe space" for student-to-student dialogue within the school; analyzing ways in which religions are portrayed in broadcast media; the Internet and school textbooks; issues concerned with the classification, description, and incorporation of "nonreligious convictions"; issues and debates concerning human rights; guidance on developing policy and practice on linking schools to local communities and organizations and developing local, national and international contacts with other schools. The closing chapter deals with further discussion and action. Again, a lot of inspiring examples from practices from various countries are included. In addition to the *Reference Book* and *Toledo*, *Signposts* offers an extensive theoretical and practical chapter on dialogue and reflection in order to improve "distancing" (a term from the *Reference Book*). *Signposts* also advocates the introduction of people from various religions into the classroom and excursions to places of interest in order to connect to the wider context of the school, especially to communities and organizations.

1.4. HERMENEUTICAL APPROACH IN EUROPE AND THE CHALLENGE OF HERMENEUTICAL JUGGLING

The situation of religious diversity in Europe and the ongoing secularization and individualization of religion challenge worldview educators, school boards, and educational policy-makers to find new ways to provide worldview education, serving the development of students and honoring human rights. Students are on

---

14. CoE, *Signposts*, 21.

European Challenges for Worldview Education

the one hand more and more religiously illiterate and on the other hand active learning subjects, constructing their own worldview identity in dialogue with peers, parents, and teachers, with religious and nonreligious worldviews, with sources of meaning taken from media and culture. Worldview educators have to adapt their aims and didactics to these facts when they want to help students to develop a worldview identity of their own, not necessarily the same as the identity of the teacher, or the school or the church providing the education. Moreover, they want to prepare their students to live in a religiously diverse and complex society with a well-rooted identity of their own, but also with a capacity to understand and converse respectfully with people that have other identities to be able to build a peaceful community together.

One of these new roads is a hermeneutical-communicative approach to worldview education. This approach recognizes that diversity is not something out there, but like the *Reference Book* concludes:

> Whether schools are secular, denominational or faith based, they all share certain features:
> —there is no real homogenous group of students, even within the same religious tradition, since religious practices and beliefs differ from one family to another and from one individual to another;
> —in modern society there are different ways of conceiving what constitutes a "good" life, and these conceptions arise from various religious and non-religious views;
> —children do not leave their values and deeply felt convictions outside when they enter the classroom. Neither children nor adults can be asked to abandon a large part of their dynamic identity in order to form a relationship with others.[15]

Pollefeyt, following Lombaerts and Maex, formulated an advocated answer to the ongoing secularization, detraditionalization

---

15. CoE, *Religious Diversity*, 15.

and deinstitutionalization in Belgian society.¹⁶ His model is a response to the question of how the school can teach worldview education in a religiously and culturally diverse society without losing its own denominational identity. Although he developed his model in a Roman Catholic context, it can easily be adopted in countries where other religions are culturally dominant or even in totally secular contexts, because of its open approach to denominations and religions. He uses the term *tradition* in a dynamic way, as internally plural and open to a world of sometimes conflicting interpretations. Far from seeing the Christian religion as an objective source of meaning, he advocates an intersubjective approach of making sense out of the differences in opinion in oneself, the classroom, the school, the church, and society when it comes to interpreting values and beliefs.

Pollefeyt identifies himself with the hermeneutical movement of recent pedagogics of religion in which worldview education is seen as a search for meaning. This movement of hermeneutics is rooted in Catholic and Protestant theology from the mid-twentieth century and associated with names like Halbfas and Tillich. According to Mette, their line of reasoning is:

> If school education aims at helping young people to gain an understanding of themselves and the world they live in, and if these young people are supposed to be enabled to act in a responsible way with regard to humanity and the world, then they also need to be familiar with the traditions that created and influenced our modern understanding of the world and humanity. By making Christianity and the biblical tradition the subject matter of interest, worldview education is therefore a great contribution to "enlightening the existence" of adolescents.¹⁷

Students are guided in formulating life questions and are confronted with wisdom from religious and nonreligious traditions in

---

16. See Pollefeyt, *Difference Matters*; *Difference of Alterity*; *Reader Course Didactics*; Lombaerts, *Hermeneutical-Communicative Concept*; Maex, *Een Hermeneutisch-Communicatief Concept*.

17. Mette, *Emergence of Hermeneutics*, 60.

order to write and rewrite their own life philosophy and to support their life stories. Truth is deconstructed, and worldview is reconstructed with building blocks from tradition and experience and in confrontation with the teacher's synthesis of his tradition.

Within a Roman Catholic educational context, Pollefeyt refers most of the time to the Christian—Catholic—tradition and to the teacher as firmly rooted in that tradition. However, in the context of other European countries, teachers prefer to use a multiplicity of traditions as sources for constructing a life philosophy. Depending on the identity of the school, the role of possible churches involved, and the personal convictions of the teacher, one or more religious or philosophical sources are offered as a mirror or as a stumbling block fostering a process of dialogue and personal reflection. Where Protestant Christian schools may choose the Bible stories or Christian feasts as the main sources for connecting experiences and convictions to the wisdom of traditions, the public schools will probably draw from socialistic, humanistic, or liberal sources, or choose to always offer more than one religious source.

Hermeneutical intersections are the keys to the learning process, according to Pollefeyt. Instead of starting from material from the Christian tradition, for instance a Bible story, one starts with the actual frames of reference from the students in the classroom. The tensions in interpretation of a certain theme or subject bring the multiplicity of possible viewpoints and the underlying traditions to the fore. Through dialogical communication, these viewpoints and sources are exposed and critically deconstructed. Pollefeyt states:

> The purpose of such a form of hermeneutical worldview education is to allow students to discover their own and others' religious/ideological presuppositions and to heighten such awareness. In this way students can become receptive to the wonderment and multifaceted interpretable character of reality. As a result, they obtain building blocks hewn from a multiplicity of religious or ideological traditions and the particular perspectives of meaning connected thereto. They learn to deal with the freedom of choice generated by this plural supply of

Learning for Life

meaning. Some religious/ideological perspectives and traditions need to be deconstructed, yet there must also be room for the (re)construction of one's life story with the newly added building materials from traditions and experiences. Ultimately, students must be able to communicate their choices to themselves and to others in words, deeds, signs and symbols.[18]

More than as an approach or a perspective, the relationship between hermeneutics and worldview education can be described as a hermeneutic condition.[19] Tradition is not in itself true, but will only be accepted by students if it can be interpreted as meaningful for them in their situation. In order to be able to mediate between tradition and the contemporary situation in education, a threefold hermeneutics is needed: the teacher must be able to use a hermeneutical method in explaining historical sources like sacred texts; the teacher needs the ability to interpret students' experiences in their contemporary societal, religious, and cultural context; and students' worldview development can be seen as hermeneutics of an active subject. The religious educator is a hermeneutic juggler, balancing these threefold hermeneutics in his didactics in order to foster the students' search for meaning and to support their personal construction of a religious identity in responding to several sources of meaning. It is this threefold hermeneutical juggling we use in our hermeneutical-communicative model in our Dutch project entitled *Learning for Life*.

---

18. Pollefeyt, *Reader Course Didactics*, 11–12.
19. Schweitzer, *Hermeneutical Condition*, 73–87.

Chapter 2
The Dutch Challenge

Developments in Worldview Education

THE EUROPEAN CHALLENGE IS also a Dutch challenge. In this chapter we address some Dutch specifics and we answer the question of how Dutch schools respond to the societal developments of secularization and pluralization in worldviews.

2.1. POST-PILLARIZED EDUCATION IN A SECULARIZED AND PLURALIZED CONTEXT

Looking at the Dutch situation concerning religious education we have to differentiate between *public* and *private* (most of the time *religious*) schools. The subject of religious education is being approached differently within these two educational varieties. However, both are subsidized in the same way. Government control exists on the quality of education within both educational varieties, but not on the religious content of religious education. The government does not prescribe a curriculum, and private schools have freedom—within the boundaries of the constitution—to appoint teachers of their preference.

In *public* schools the teaching of religion is optional: parents can demand worldview education for their children about their own religion, and they can choose Catholic, Protestant, Islamic, or Humanistic lessons. Public schools have the duty to provide these lessons, mostly carried out by teachers from these religious groups. Public schools are expected to actively stimulate pluriformity, to prepare children to live in a diverse society. In 1985 the *Dutch Primary Education Act* was accepted by the parliament. This act prescribes that all schools, public as well as private, need to adopt a subject in their curriculum called "Geestelijke Stromingen" (ideological and spiritual movements), in which objective information on a variety of religious and secular worldviews needs to be offered. All schools, private and public, have to inform children about "spiritual movements" in an "objective" way: teaching about. Most of the private schools, being religious schools, incorporate this course in their curriculum of religious education.

In *private* schools, participating in religious education is compulsory. From a sociological standpoint we can best describe the current Dutch situation in *private* schools as "post-pillarized." Previously this education used to neatly fit the different dominant religious traditions (Roman Catholic, Protestant Christian, Reformed, Jewish) and both teachers and students tended to belong to the same pillar. The aims for religious education were fairly straightforward: to initiate students into the beliefs, rituals, and practices of the dominant tradition and to its church(es). Today, these denominations are still found, but the situation has become more complex and in some cases less clear. Teachers as well as students are, when it comes to worldview, strongly influenced by processes of secularization, individualization, pluralization, multiculturalization, and detraditionalization. These processes have been increasing in force since the 1970s and did not halt at the doors of Christian schools.

The times they are changing. Until 1960, in the Netherlands eight out of ten inhabitants professed to belong to one of the Christian denominations. In 1970, 75% of all Dutch people were registered as members of one Christian community or another. In 2005, thirty-five years later, that number had decreased to 45% and it is expected that, in 2020, nearly 75% of the entire Dutch

The Dutch Challenge

population will no longer belong to any of the church communities.[1] Society depillarizes quickly and this can be noticed in Dutch education. In 1966, 55% of parents still sent their children to a primary school that belonged to "their" pillar. By 2002, that number had shrunk to 34%. Until 1960, in the pillarized Dutch society, the function of religious education at private schools revolved around the initiation of students into a certain religious tradition. The parents played an important role at nearly all Christian schools (e.g., as members of the school board).[2] At the public schools, religion and worldview education were discussed at the request of parents and the curriculum surrounding Christianity, Islam, or humanist worldview were mostly based on the transfer of information.

Parents' motives for sending their children to Christian schools have become more diverse. The distance between home and school, the influence parents have on the school board, and public values professed to be held by the schools (such as mutual respect between students) are now reasons for nonreligious parents to enroll their children in Christian schools.[3] Furthermore, the receptivity in schools to a variety of worldviews and orientations plays a deciding role in the choice parents make. A considerable amount of confessional schools present themselves as an open school: open to parents and children who are rooted in different worldview traditions.

Depillarization and a Newfound Interest in Meaning

In response to these societal, cultural, and philosophical developments, we see a variety of standpoints emerge in the Netherlands regarding religious education, approaches, and aims.[4] The Netherlands is on its way to becoming a post-pillarized society while religiosity and spirituality at the same time remain themes

---

1. Becker and De Hart, *Godsdienstige Veranderingen in Nederland*; Bernts and Berghuijs, *God in Nederland, 1966–2015*.
2. Onderwijsraad, *Samen Leren Leven*.
3. Dijkstra et al., *Verzuiling in het Onderwijs*.
4. Geurts et al., *Religious Education in the Netherlands*.

to which both youths and adults are attracted. In late-modern society, people construct their own outlook on both humanity and the world as a whole. According to De Hart, a self-constructed religious identity reflects both the religious fragmentation at the social level and the spiritual desire for people to find meaning in their lives and to find a value-laden lifestyle at the subjective level.[5] The statistics from the survey *God in Nederland* (God in the Netherlands) are clear: two-thirds of the Dutch people do not attend church and a large part of the population no longer turns to religion when it comes to matters of sense making.[6] This means that existing religious institutions are losing their influence on the majority of the people.

People now shape their own worldviews. One could say that religion as we have always known it is transforming; it is becoming more and more adaptable to individuals. When it comes to sense making, people pick and choose what they believe fits their own lives and questions best. The wide variety of sources that can serve a purpose in the process of sense making is now situated in the public space: apart from institutions such as churches and monasteries, there now are television programs, magazines, and books pertaining to spirituality, philosophy, religion, and meaning; there are cultural phenomena such as film, theatre, literature, and art. Then, there is the internet, which offers a vast array of sources from which people can construct knowledge and insights. People choose for themselves how they wish to lead their lives and what they find important. They do so fairly autonomously, but naturally they do so in accordance with their own environment and the groups they belong to, the networks they partake in. That does not mean that traditions no longer play a role in sense making; it simply means that their authority no longer goes without saying. Traditions (beliefs, texts, rituals, moral codes) are only adopted in relation to the extent to which they are or become meaningful in a person's life. This individualization also means that people tend to employ elements from various different traditions and find or

5. De Hart, *Zwevende Gelovigen*.
6. Bernts and Berghuijs, *God in Nederland, 1966–2015*.

The Dutch Challenge

discover meaning in various situations. In doing so, people tend not to be impressed by the matter of whether these beliefs stemming from different sources are in line with one another: as long as it "works," as long as it helps, as long as it adds profundity to life, it makes sense to someone. People make all kinds of combinations; they try out different things and occasionally engage with multiple traditions at the same time (double belonging). People's worldviews are becoming somewhat of a patchwork, a bricolage.

The term next to individualization is "pluralization": the autonomous structuring of worldview identity both within and outside of religious contexts allows for a wide variety of stances. Not all Christians believe and live in the same way and the same holds for other religions. This worldview or religious plurality or worldview diversity is even more noticeable among the two-thirds of all Dutch people who no longer consider themselves to be a part of a religious tradition. The multitude of outlooks and practices causes the Netherlands to wildly vary when it comes to worldviews: whether it is in the context of rituals, moral codes, or the relation to God, life, and death, no outlook or practice is absolute or applicable to all. For instance, "God" can mean the Heavenly Father to one, but at the same time be a dynamic force of love uniting people to another, or a meaningless artifact stashed away in one of grandfather's boxes to a third. The teacher is tasked with dealing with this extremely varied current state of affairs.

In primary schools, the adopted stance toward worldview education is shifting, which is influenced by this process of modernization, expressed in individualization and pluralization. Modernization during late-modernity impacts, among other things, the ways in which people think about the meaning of religious and philosophical traditions. Traditions are no longer considered to be closed systems of beliefs transferred with authority from generation to generation, but rather as sources which late-modern people can use freely to construct a personal view of both humanity and the world. This transition in the perception of traditions is also made visible in the ways in which worldviews are taught in both private and public schools.

Learning for Life

This shift can be perceived in public schools primarily through a new mode of thinking emerging at those schools about the ways in which students are raised to function in a multireligious society. Apart from clear nonreligious or on occasion antireligious stances or a so-called neutral stance, we observe an increasing positive interest in the subjects of worldviews and religion, and some public schools embrace the notion that one of the tasks set out for public education is to familiarize the students with the various worldviews.[7] From a pedagogical point of view, public schools need to be allotted more freedom to develop a practice of active plurality than is currently the case within the strict interpretation of "neutrality" in public education.[8]

The close relation between the three parties which until the 1960s were involved in Dutch religious education—family, school, and church—has been dissolved by depillarization. This led to a wide variety of stances on education and, specifically, on worldview education and ultimately to the careful introduction of new practices. The deconstruction of the pillarized education system allows room for the reconstruction of religious education within the context of a multicultural society. New pedagogical-didactic competences for teachers will be required to shape a new form of worldview education in which the questions and realities of students are centralized and in which the students' curiosity to explore the many existing traditions is stimulated. The dismantling of the triangular relationship of family, church, and school ultimately led to a new perspective on the relevance of the knowledge of other religious and philosophical traditions at many confessional schools. This in turn effected the way in which the subject "Geestelijke Stromingen" was taught and led to the conceptualization of small-scale experiments surrounding philosophical education in which

7. VOSS/ABB plays an active part in generating attention for worldviews in public education, for instance through their distribution of flyers titled *Levensbeschouwing JUIST in het openbaar onderwijs*, https://www.vosabb.nl/wp-content//uploads/2016/02/Brochure-levensbeschouwing-juist-in-het-openbaar-onderwijs-VO-webversie.pdf.

8. Onderwijsraad, *Artikel 23*. Bakker, *Levensbeschouwelijk Onderwijs voor Alle Leerlingen*.

the philosophical development of each individual student was centralized.

2.2. CURRENT PRACTICES IN DUTCH WORLDVIEW EDUCATION: TWO PRIMARY SCHOOLS

To outline the current practice at private (confessional) schools, we will describe the social-cultural, pedagogic-didactic, and religious-philosophical practices on two regular primary schools in the Netherlands, named De Polsstok and De Wonderboom.[9]

Social-Cultural Context

Primary school De Polsstok is a school with a religious foundation, which is part of the *DE Brede School*, a coalition of three primary schools in Southeast Amsterdam.[10] The concept of a "Brede" (broad) school is developed in collaboration with the As Soefa school (an Islamic primary school) and the Bijlmerhorst (a public primary school). On October 1, 2009, 318 students were enrolled at De Polsstok, distributed among eighteen classes. Each class consists of students with a wide variety of ethnical, cultural, and religious backgrounds. In this way, De Polsstok states in the delineation of its vision, the school aims to offer each individual student a safe space to learn, but also to challenge them to grow up to be an open-minded and dedicated member of a global society. Its staff consists of twenty-two employees and the team reflects the

---

9. De Polsstok can be translated as *The Jumping Pole* and De Wonderboom as *The Miracle Tree*. The description refers to the situation in 2009 and many schools of today can recognize this situation.

10. De Polsstok is not a traditional Protestant Christian school. It is a member of *Stichting Bijzonderwijs*, a coalition of ten primary schools which consider themselves to be *ecumenical primary schools*. In 2003, the shift was made from *ecumenical* to *philosophical*, which allowed for a better expression of the diversity of worldview backgrounds in the team, among parents, and among students.

Learning for Life

multicolored structure of the school-going population of Southeast Amsterdam.

Primary school De Wonderboom is situated in the Nieuwland neighborhood of Amersfoort and has three locations. The first, called "Waterkers," consists of groups 1 to 3; the second, "Zeldertse Dreef," of groups 4 and 5 and one mixed group of fifth- and sixth-year students; and the third location, "De Bonte Koe," consists of groups 6, 7, and 8. In total, De Wonderboom counts over six hundred students. Around fifty people work there, who once again reflect the student population and general population of Nieuwland in Amersfoort, which is diverse. The team believes it is important for all students to be seen and acknowledged for their uniqueness.

Pedagogic-Didactic Practices

In De Polsstok, the motto is as follows: "The plural of together is future." The DE Brede schools aim to improve education, students' learning accomplishments, and the societal perspective of both students and parents. At DE Brede, schools, parents, and supporting organizations collaborate in healthcare, wellbeing, sport and culture. All four- to twelve-year-old children are welcomed. Furthermore, De Polsstok pays close attention to new insights that could improve education. This way, it expects to "mold students into people who can contribute to society in a positive way."[11] This quote, which originates from the document in which the vision of De Polsstok is outlined, shows that its team is aware of the vulnerability of the social-economic and social-cultural infrastructure of its surroundings, hence its emphasis on the personal and social development of each student.

The aim of De Wonderboom is to be a learning community that consists of young people and their tutors. Learning is not only focused at cognitive growth; the complete development of each child is the focal point. Good education, according to the school,

11. See the document outlining the vision of De Polsstok at www.polsstok.nl; Ter Avest and Clement, *Samen School Maken in de Bijlmer*.

The Dutch Challenge

factors in the developmental demands of each individual child. In class, the teachers emphasize the students' cooperation with one another. This means that the students learn to work together through various teaching formats. This way, they are actively engaged in the learning process. In the document outlining the vision of De Wonderboom, the school states that students, by collaborating with their peers, can discover many things about themselves and others, develop their social skills, and improve their learning performances.[12] At De Wonderboom, a kind of equilibrium is sought between good results at school and the students' personal growth. In 2011, the school fine-tuned its vision, which is now phrased as follows: "respecting uniqueness, learning to claim ownership and to pay close attention to your own way."[13]

Religious-Philosophical Practices

Both schools employ a teaching method for religious and worldview education, the approach of which could in theory facilitate the desired transition of the model of knowledge transferal toward a model in which the cooperative investigation and exploration of philosophical questions, themes, and sources is centralized. However, the room to maneuver within the methods employed has as of yet not led to a practice of worldview education in which the student is the subject.[14] Instead, at many primary schools, said practice remains limited to moments such as the ritual opening and closing of the day, when children listen to a biblical narrative or partake in minor ritual acts (a prayer, a song, etc.). Only a few

---

12. See the document outlining the vision of De Wonderboom at www.wonderboom.pcboamersfoort.nl.

13. Schoolgids Wonderboom, 2011–2012 and 2012–2013.

14. At De Polsstok, the method *Hemel & Aarde* is used and the method *Trefwoord* is used at De Wonderboom. *Hemel & Aarde* seeks to find a balance between on the one hand the familiarization of students with rich worldview traditions and on the other hand their own exploration of lived traditions. A clear vision on the philosophical development of students lies at its core. At the core of *Trefwoord* lies a vision regarding philosophical learning and worldview development which emphasizes the transferal of knowledge.

Learning for Life

practices have surfaced in which philosophical learning in which the student is centralized has manifested itself in structured activities throughout the day.[15]

The philosophy at De Polsstok is to offer quality education to all children, regardless of their cultural or religious backgrounds. In each classroom, there are students and a teacher coming from various religious traditions (such as Christian, Islamic, Hindu) and various cultural traditions (Surinamese, African, Arab, and Dutch). In their teaching of worldviews, the teachers emphasize the equality of all traditions and promote respect for all children and teachers, as is in line with the document outlining the school's vision. To raise and to teach children is, according to the school, to allow the child and its talents to flourish in every way possible, including on a philosophical level. At De Polsstok, worldview education is shaped by themes originating from the teaching method *Hemel en Aarde* (heaven and earth). Most teachers start out the day using this method, but they are also free to do so at any other moment during the day. At De Polsstok, holidays from various religions are celebrated.[16] An "identity counselor" provides the teachers with guidance on how to work with the themes from *Hemel en Aarde*.

De Wonderboom has a more general Christian foundation. According to the document outlining its vision, the school subscribes to the notion that all children are created in God's likeness, meaning that all children are good and complete the way they are. All teachers start the day with a theme from *Trefwoord* (key word), a commonly used method for religious education on Protestant primary schools.[17] This is frequently done by way of telling a narrative accompanied by a song or a prayer. In particular, the holidays of Easter and Christmas are celebrated extensively. Through these

15. In the research track at public and special schools in the province of Zeeland (2009–2011), examples of a new practice have been made visible. See Parlevliet et al., *Het Kind en de Grote Verhalen*.

16. Festivities celebrated are the Diwali festival, Eid al-Fitr, Purim, and Easter.

17. The method *Trefwoord* was originally created for Protestant Christian education.

celebrations, the children can experience the meaning of these festivities. Holidays belonging to other worldviews are not celebrated at all. The Bible is the sole source used by De Wonderboom when it comes to the philosophical development of its students. The population of De Wonderboom—its teachers and students—is mixed. At this school, there is a tension between teachers and students with a Christian background and those with a secular worldview. The school acknowledges this diversity and attempts to include respect toward and an understanding of people with different beliefs and worldviews in its teaching method, without sacrificing its prioritization of the Christian tradition as a source of inspiration.[18]

2.3. AN EMPOWERING LEARNING ENVIRONMENT FOR WORLDVIEW EDUCATION

One of the effects of depillarization of the Dutch worldview education practice is the challenge to rethink pedagogics and didactics of religious education. What many schools together with De Wonderboom en De Polsstok need is to develop an empowering learning environment, in which plurality is honored and respect and understanding are fostered, starting from the development of all the children as a focal point. At the two described primary schools, a discrepancy can generally be perceived between new forms of collaborative and creative learning in subjects such as language, mathematics, and world studies and the lack thereof in developmental areas such as cultural education and religious and worldview education. Whereas a powerful learning environment is established for other subjects, for example using principles from cooperative learning (CL) or narrative design (ND), we have observed that this hardly happens in the case of cultural education and religious and worldview education. The focal point of the learning process in schools is shifting toward an increasingly widespread approach in which subjects are explored more and more in context by students. Students are now trained to construct knowledge in

18. See the vision regarding philosophical education and identity development described in the vision document of De Wonderboom.

a rich learning environment, which provides for their personal needs and is connected to their personal world. Since 1985, this constructivist approach to learning has been combined with a phenomenological and hermeneutic approach, both in theory and in practice. The learning process starts out with existential questions raised by students, after which a source from a religious or philosophical tradition is used as an incentive to reflect upon the students' own development of a worldview.[19] This way, students learn to inquisitively explore philosophical questions, phenomena, and sources and they learn to make sense of and find meaning in said sources. What follows is that worldview education is made meaningful within a specific context.

Current Theory on Meaningful Learning

Currently, two processes which stimulate meaningful learning can be distinguished. According to educationist K. Illeris, students come to learn meaningfully when the interaction among students themselves, between students and their social environment, and between students and the subject matter is stimulated. Another way in which this happens is by "incentives," for example through the evocation of imagery or the stimulation of curiosity regarding a subject.[20]

Until 1980, theory on learning revolved primarily around the notions of the acquisition of knowledge and the transferal of knowledge. From 1990 onward, the focus shifted toward learning being a social and interactive process between the student, his or her environment, and the subject matter. From that framework, Illeris developed a triangular model for learning in which a distinction is made between three dimensions: the dimension of contents, characterized by terms such as "knowledge," "insight," and "skills"; the dimension of "incentives," characterized by terms such as "motivation," "emotion" and "will"; and the dimension of

19. Hermans, *Participerend Leren*.
20. Illeris, *How We Learn*, 22–29.

the interaction between the learner and his or her material surroundings, characterized by terms such as "action," "communication," and "cooperation." Through the dimension of contents, the actions, familiarization, and understanding of the learner are developed and said student is enabled to develop a meaning or, in other words, a coherent insight into a certain subject matter. This dimension also helps develop the student's ability to function adequately in a variety of contexts. The dimension of incentives is what puts learning in motion. This can be done through sparking curiosity, insecurity, an emotion or a desire which challenges the learner to seek new knowledge and to acquire new skills. This dimension serves to develop the mental receptivity of the learner in relation to his or her environment. The dimensions of content and incentives bolster each other when it comes to the processes of both active and passive construction of knowledge. The content learned is always shaped by the mental energy put in motion for the sake of the learning process. The interactive dimension integrates the person as an actor into relevant contexts and communities. This dimension contributes to the social development of the learner.

Illeris's theory facilitates the differentiation between three dimensions to learning which lead to the construction of knowledge in relation to a certain subject, increase the extent to which students are involved with a certain subject, and lead to the stimulation of interaction and cooperation between students within an empowering learning environment. What is new in Illeris' theory is the connection made between students' motives for their construction of knowledge and the content about which knowledge is constructed. Through motives such as curiosity, wonder, or amazement, an emotional involvement with a certain subject is generated. This emotional involvement allows the student to familiarize him- or herself with a certain subject or to refuse to do so. The dimensions identified by Illeris can be recognized in all forms of learning in primary education. Worldview learning, too, can be described and clarified by way of this triadic model of learning. In this way, word view learning can be imagined as a process of making sense of and finding meaning within a fascinating subject through the activation of the student's ability to become curious, to become amazed, and to wonder and by challenging them to explore a subject through various forms of interaction and dialogue.

Love for Learning

In Ruijters' dissertation, *Liefde voor Leren* (Love for Learning), several key terms can be found which align closely with Illeris's three dimensions.[21] If a learning environment challenges students to cooperate and to conduct a dialogue in their exploration of a theme or source, *dialogical* or *participatory* learning is stimulated.[22] If such an environment challenges students to explore a theme or source (i.e., content) from the starting point of their own questions and curiosity, *involved* or *inquisitive* learning is stimulated.[23] Lastly, if students are challenged to create their own links between what they know and what they do not yet know, *creative* or *exploratory* learning is stimulated.[24] Illeris's and Ruijters's theories both presume a socially constructivist stance toward learning. In his model, Illeris links the acquisition of knowledge to the mental energy required to find meaning in a certain subject and to the social interaction with the learner's surroundings.[25] Based on Illeris's and Ruijters's theories outlined above, an empowering learning environment for worldview education can be described as an environment in which students are challenged to investigate a subject (a question, a theme, a source)—motivated by curiosity and armed with their imagination—to construct knowledge about that subject. A learning environment can be made challenging for students if they are stimulated to engage in dialogue with one

21. Ruijters, *Liefde voor Leren*; Ruijters and Simons, *Canon van het Leren*.

22. Ruijters, *Liefde voor Leren*; Illeris, *How We Learn*.

23. Van Oers, *Ontwikkelingsgericht Werken*; Letschert et al., *Beyond Storyline*; Egan, *Educated Mind*; Ruijters, *Liefde voor Leren*, 118–23.

24. Bruner, *Culture of Education*; Egan, *Educated Mind*; Stern, *Spirit of the School*.

25. Illeris, *How We Learn*, 27.

The Dutch Challenge

another and with the subject matter through their investigation of a worldview phenomenon and if they are activated to interpret the subject creatively through curiosity and imagination to make sense and find meaning in it.

Dialogical, Creative, and Investigative Learning

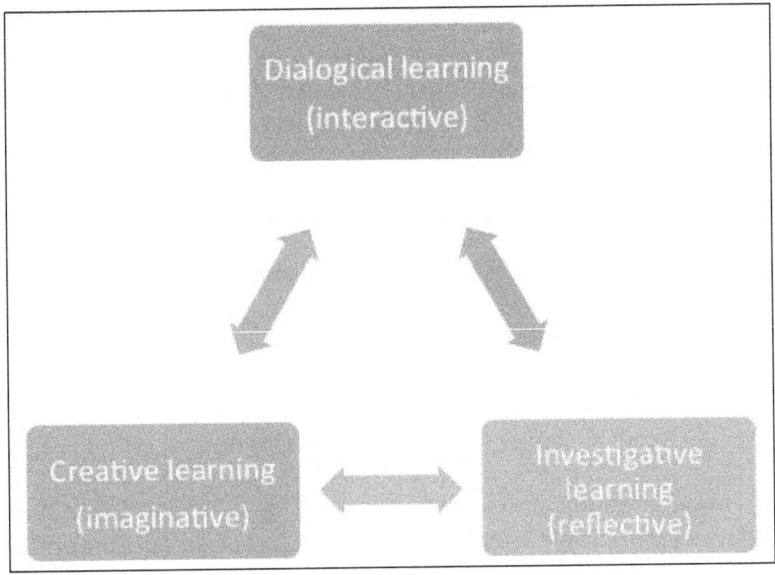

Figure 1. The Three Dimensions of Learning in the Educational Margin: "Dialogical Learning" (Interactive), "Investigative Learning" (Reflective), and "Creative Learning" (Creative)

In Dutch (religious) pedagogical theory development, dialogical learning (also described as *participatory* or *interactive* learning) was first described by, among others, Hermans and Schaap.[26] In his realization of the concept *participatory learning*, Hermans primarily uses theories from Vygotsky and Bakhtin. He believes that participatory learning can be described as a way of learning in which students take part in *religious practices* to make sense and find meaning. In Hermans's studies, Bakhtin features most

26. Hermans, *Participerend Leren*; Schaap, *Pedagogiek van Zingeving*.

prominently when the *dialogical aspect* of participatory learning is discussed. Schaap has investigated the principles of interactive or dialogical learning over the course of several research studies in a very early stage. He can be seen as the founder of this approach in the Netherlands, already in the 1990s. Philosophical learning as a means to acquire knowledge has a long history in religious-pedagogical research.[27] In such research, relatively little attention is paid, however, to *creative* and *investigative* learning as described by Ruijters and Simons, following Sfard.[28] In learning as creating and investigating, the emphasis is on the development of *creativity* in students, on the bolstering of their capabilities when it comes to wonder and imagination and on their mental and social abilities such as playing and creating. Characteristics of creative/investigative learning are discussed in research into students' creative and interactive learning conducted by, among others, Egan, Eisner, and Letschert.[29]

The Hermeneutical-Communicative Approach in the Netherlands

In our exploration of what an empowering environment for worldview learning could look like, we learn that such an environment should stimulate dialogical, investigative, and creative processes. In this environment, students are encouraged to engage in interaction, creativity, and reflection, which allows them to make sense of and find meaning, both alone and together, through exploring an existential question, a worldview theme or source. Philosophical learning at primary schools can become empowering for students when interaction and dialogue among students and between students and a certain subject is intensified and when their creativity and curiosity is sparked.

---

27. Alii, *Godsdienstpedagogiek*.
28. Ruijters and Simons, *Canon van het Leren*.
29. Egan, *Educated Mind*; Egan, *Imaginative Approach*.

The Dutch Challenge

Teachers in primary education are confronted with the results of depillarization, individualization, and pluralization on a daily basis. Over the course of the final decades of the twentieth century, worldview education was already seen from a wider perspective and with a more open mind toward various religious and worldview perspectives.

Many Dutch scholars follow Pollefeyt's pedagogical vision on worldview education in which the differences in religious and worldview background form the incentives for encounter between students and for the development of a religious identity. These so-called hermeneutical intersections lead to exploration and discussion.[30] In *Godsdienstpedagogiek* (Pedagogy of Religious Education) the aforementioned perspectives are conjoined and practical applications are provided.[31] The depillarization of the Dutch society, the modernization and the transformation of religion have changed religious education from a practice which served to support the initiation of a homogenous group of students into one tradition to a praxis in which existential questions raised by students are hermeneutically explored, with the help of the hermeneutic of meaningful sources from worldview and religion and in dialogue with each other.

Over the course of the last seven years, we, as a part of the project *Learning for Life*, have tried to find alternatives for what could be described as the model of transfer within worldview education, the model in which the primary goal is to socialize children in a religious regard within a certain tradition. This model stimulates the exploration of questions raised within their current plural context when it comes to the goals and didactics of worldview education. Now that the close ties between family, school, and church have disappeared in many ways, schools search new ways in which to connect with the once dominant Christian tradition and its representatives, to get in touch with other religious traditions and to form new relations between parents and teachers within newer worldview approaches.

30. See chapter 1.
31. Alii, *Godsdienstpedagogiek*.

Learning for Life

This search for alternatives was manifested in two government funded RAAK research projects: *Het Kind en de Grote Verhalen* (*The Child and the Grand Narratives*, 2010–2012) and *Leren voor het Leven* (*Learning for Life*, 2014–2016). The doctoral research of one of the authors, *Speelruimte voor Dialoog en Verbeelding* (2008–2014), ran parallel to these projects.[32] The focal point of both projects was to stage the worldview development of each individual student as the primary goal of worldview education. In this instance, "each" refers to every possible realization of students' own vision or way of life. We believe every school, whether it is public or private in whichever form, has the mandate to guide children in their search for answers to both major and minor existential questions. Every school can do so in their own way and in accordance with their own identity, but there should always be room for the individual uniqueness of the child. In *Het Kind en de Grote Verhalen*, a hermeneutic-communicative perspective on worldview education was employed that was developed by Didier Pollefeyt and expanded by us to fit the new societal reality in a post-pillarized society.[33]

Educating Worldviews

We believe that worldview education should aim at the personal exploration of meaning of each individual student. Finding meaning enables students to place their thoughts, experiences, and actions within a larger context, whether it be cognitively, emotionally, or through actions. When life does not appear to show meaning or does not allow itself to be experienced naturally, worldviews can help a person find their way in life, to seek the bigger context and—however fleetingly—to discover it. To us, a worldview encapsulates a unity of insights, values, beliefs, images, and experiences that is traditionally shaped and handed down in narrative form and which is usually expressed by way of characteristic

32. Van den Berg, *Speelruimte*.

33. Parlevliet et al., *Het Kind en de Grote Verhalen*; Van den Berg and Mulder, *Leren van Betekenis*.

rituals and habits. Worldviews offer outlooks, life styles, narratives, and (occasionally) rituals which serve to experience meaning. In conjunction with the theory about learning, we can also state that each worldview has material, mental, and social dimensions. In his religious studies, N. Smart has shown that seven dimensions can be identified for each worldview: a narrative dimension, a ritual one, a social one, a material one, an idealistic one, a moral one, and an existential one.[34]

Worldviews are varied: there are religious ones (such as Islam, Christianity, Hinduism, Judaism) as well as nonreligious ones (humanism, liberalism). These two variants can, of course, then be divided once more: they can either be institutionalized or non-institutionalized; the first is materialized by way of institutions such as a church, a mosque, a temple, and so on, whereas the second is more personal and more detached from such institutions. For example, there are agnostic Jews and Christians with "patchwork worldviews," but also dedicated atheist humanists or hedonistic agnostics. The core of a worldview is a more or less coherent whole of beliefs and attitudes through which one's own experiences can be judged and directed. This wide interpretation of worldview is what we use in our hermeneutic-communicative model of worldview education. We believe and have experienced that this interpretation can be applied to both Christian and secular education, no matter the diversity.

While a teacher aims to unite students with one singular tradition within the model of transfer, a multitude of traditions and sources are used to foster the worldview development of students in our hermeneutic-communicative model. In this model, differences between students when it comes to insight are not to be discouraged, but instead they should be seen as a starting point for students to get to know one another as well as the sources in a new light. Through dialogue, they also get to know themselves and their own background better. Apart from recognizing this plurality, Pollefeyt and the other authors also acknowledge the individualization perceived in society as being a worthy challenge for

34. Smart, *World's Religions*.

worldview education; they consider it a tool to be used in the student's personal search for a meaningful existence. In other words, worldview education should contribute to the personal philosophical construction of identity of all students.[35] Or, in the words of the pedagogue Robert Jackson: "Religious education is a series of existential and social debates in which students are encouraged to participate, with a personal stake related to their own developing sense of identity ... a process in which students, whether from 'secular' or 'religious' backgrounds, continuously interpret and reinterpret their own views in the light of their studies."[36] In our next chapter we will demonstrate our hermeneutical-communicative model which integrates our learning theory with our hermeneutical perspective on dialogical and student-centered worldview education.

---

35. Pollefeyt, *Reader Course Didactics*.
36. Jackson, *Rethinking*, 17–18.

Chapter 3
Learning for Life

A Hermeneutical-Communicative Model for Worldview Education

THE MODEL WE DEVELOPED in our *Learning for Life* project draws heavily on the work of Pollefeyt, and on recent developments in theory on hermeneutics as summarized in the previous chapters. It is our answer to the religious and educational challenges of the situation in the Netherlands of today. In this chapter, we will present the four elements of the model: the goals, the didactical roles, the faculties of students, and the dimensions of worldviews. We will illustrate the model with some examples.

3.1. HERMENEUTICAL-COMMUNICATIVE LEARNING

The hermeneutical-communicative compound which Pollefeyt and his colleagues of the University of Leuven use points to the heart of the theoretical perspective on worldview education as a learning process.

Hermeneutical means that the teacher aims at the interpretation of sources of meaning in worldview education in connection

Learning for Life

to the lives of the students. The teacher is always focused on what presents itself as meaningful in the stories of students, in the perceived experiences of the students, and in the traditions or sources they know and live by. We use sources and traditions in plural because the pluralistic society implies that the worldview educator cannot depart from only one meaningful source to correlate with the questions and life stories of students. Mono-correlation—in the direction of the Bible as the only source in searching for meaning must be replaced by multi-correlation to do justice to religious diversity in society, in the homes of children, in the classroom, and more and more in teacher populations. We concur with Pollefeyt in his view that people are hermeneutical creatures, looking for meaning and open to wisdom conveyed by traditions.[1] The hermeneutical condition implies that life is open to multiple interpretations, and so are the sources of meaning people use for guidance in their lives. There is no such a thing as "the" Christian tradition or "the" Islamic tradition. Traditions are pluralistic by their nature. An exchange is therefore always necessary. Here we come to the second word in the *hermeneutical-communicative* compound.

Communicative means that the teacher aims at dialogical exchange of views and experiences in the encounter with students about what is meaningful to them. This exchange starts with an open attitude from the teacher, with a real interest in the stories of the students. The teacher recognizes his own reactions and reflects on them to the students in a respectful way. The teacher is willing to share his views and experiences to reach mutual understanding. By eliciting the opinions and stories and moderating discussions and conversations between students, a dialogue can take place. Differences of opinion between students come to light, and they are used as a starting point for a deep learning process. Conflicting interpretations of reality and of sources of meaning are laid bare and traced back to suppositions about reality, world, God, and so on. In these conversations, students and teacher may change their views or attitude regarding the subject at hand. Worldview

---

1. Pollefeyt, *Reader: Course Didactics—Imparting Life*, 10–13, and *Reader: Course Didactics—The Lustre of Life*, 1–4.

education never is a one-way street.² Worldview education is, in our view, not only and not foremost the transmission of meaningful information, but particularly the construction of meaning in interaction.

Movements

In shorthand, we can describe the hermeneutical-communicative approach in several movements:

- *From instruction to interpretation.* The teacher is not the all-knowing and all-wise instructor about life's goals and ethical prescriptions. Worldview education is a full-fledged collective hermeneutical enterprise. Teacher and students take a walk down discovery lane.
- *From explaining texts to threefold hermeneutics.* Teachers are juggling with the hermeneutics of religious sources, hermeneutics of context, and hermeneutics of personal existence. In the classroom, worldview education tries to offer a safe place where existential questions can be formulated and discussed and where the sociocultural and political dimensions of the students' context are analyzed. Although the interpretation of sacred texts will still be important, worldview education is seen as more fruitful when this hermeneutic of texts is linked to and combined with the other two: the existential and contextual hermeneutics.
- *From mono-religious to inter-worldview education.* With the waning of Christian influence in Dutch society and the growing cultural and religious diversity in the classrooms, worldview education has to honor multiple perspectives on fundamental issues to serve all the students. Especially the arrival of Muslim immigrants from Turkey and Morocco and the immigration of adherents of Hinduism from the former Dutch colony of Suriname in the twentieth century have

2. Dillen, *Religious Participation*, 44.

changed the religious landscape of the Netherlands forever. Students must learn to live in a multireligious context. The task of the school is to prepare the students for the religiously plural society and to provide a powerful learning environment in which they can develop their personal worldview identity. The best preparation for such a society is to encounter the multiple religions present today.

- *From teaching into to teaching about and from religion.* A consequence of the colorful palette of values and beliefs present in the students in our classrooms is that the task of initiation is left to the church and other religious institutions. There is a difference between religious nurturing and worldview education. However, it is only possible to contribute to the goal of forming a worldview identity in education if students are able to receive information and to experience religious rituals or artifacts and possibly respond to them. Religions, life philosophies, and wisdom in popular culture are all seen as important sources. Education must be more than transfer of concepts: it must also be a critical examination of phenomena and a personal appropriation of these phenomena. This means not only that students will become more religiously literate (their knowledge about religions will increase) but also that they will be more religiously competent in dialogue and personal response to religious content. Religious and philosophical traditions are not only there to know but also to grow.

- *From convincing to witnessing.* The majority of schools in the Netherlands are private and Christian in origin, funded either by Christian associations or foundations, or by churches. Teachers may have chosen to be a Christian teacher at a Christian school to have the opportunity to bring children to Jesus, to spread the gospel. Especially ritual moments or hours of worldview education offer an opportunity to share the truth about life, sin, and redemption and to try to convince the children of biblical principles. However, in a plural classroom, with children who are in many cases not sent to this school for religious reasons but for reasons of convenience or quality standards, teachers cannot—if they could ever—have the aim of proselytizing. They have to change focus to witnessing. The same is true for an atheist or agnostic teacher at a public school.

- *From teacher-centeredness or tradition-centeredness to student-centeredness.* In a hermeneutical approach, students' questions and their interpretive responses to material from sources of wisdom—be it traditional or drawn from popular culture—take center stage. The activities of the teacher and the encounter with religious materials are both at the service of the student's development of a religious identity.

3.2. THE HERMENEUTICAL-COMMUNICATIVE MODEL

Our hermeneutical-communicative model has four aspects: (1) Starting from the questions of the student, we formulate three learning objectives. (2) We keep the learning faculties of the students in mind. (3) We offer a multiplicity of worldview sources following Ninian Smart. (4) We present four didactical roles.

3.2.1. Aims of Hermeneutical-Communicative Worldview Education

Following Didier Pollefeyt and Robert Jackson, we stress that the development of the student is the core business of worldview education. All efforts are in service of the student's development in terms of worldview. Education aims to contribute to the growth into adulthood of unique human beings. Every student works on his life project, life vision, spirituality, or belief. The student is an actor in the construction of meaning and at the same time a receiver of meaning in a reciprocal process with significant figures in their lives like parents, caretakers, peers, and teachers, and sources of meaning. Education is responsible for the coming into presence of unique human beings, as Biesta puts it.[3] Existential questions that students have about the world, future, the other, God, the Self, nature are starting points for learning processes. From this heart of education, we formulate three aims of our model which are closely connected:

1. *Personal Clarification of Existence*: Students learn to articulate their questions and to formulate their views on living in this world, to develop their own ways of living, and to explore existential questions and life issues. They reflect on them and explore sources of meaning in dialogue with others to construct and reconstruct their own personal religious presence in the world.

2. *Dialogical Responding to Plurality*: Students develop a receptive and critical attitude in order to manage differences in how people see their lives, in interpretation of religious sources, and in the choices people make related to their worldview. Students can converse about these differences in a respectful way in order to be prepared to contribute constructively and peacefully to debates in a plural and diverse society.

3. *Worldview Literacy*: Students gain valuable insights and wisdom from the confrontation with worldview traditions as expressed and conveyed in stories, rituals, symbols, views, laws, architecture, music, art, from history as well as from today. They acquire basic knowledge about religious traditions and know how to relate to the information in a critical way and to formulate their own reactions to solutions to life issues offered in that information.

Biesta formulated three general purposes for education: subjectification, socialization, and qualification.[4] We made them specific for worldview education: by addressing existential questions of stu-

---

3. Biesta, *Good Education*, 91.
4. Biesta, *Good Education*, 20–21.

dents in an open way, the hermeneutical-communicative model contributes to subjectification. By teaching dialogical skills and a respectful attitude, the model contributes to socialization into a multicultural and multireligious democratic society. And by introducing religious content in an interactive way, students are prepared to qualify in the subject of religion and worldview.

These purposes of education obviously expect some skills from the teacher, and some conditions from the school. We shall discuss them now.

Personal Clarification of Existence

We see the formation of a religious identity primarily as a task of the individual person, of the child itself in its orientation in the world. Reflection on what is of ultimate value or ultimate concern is a constitutive part of identity formation. The child is confronted on its road of life with everything in the smaller or wider personal and cultural context. Life events, situations of wonder, and deep emotions elicit questions in the student. The child puts together a personal worldview from all kinds of sources of meaning and creates a flexible identity. The student shares her questions at home and in the classroom. Smaller and bigger questions are discussed in dialogical interaction with other significant figures. In turn, these others show what is of ultimate concern to them, which sources of meaning they use, and how they handle questions of life. It is important that the child learns a language to express feelings, thoughts, and associations in the exploration and appropriation of possible answers to the questions. Worldview education stimulates reflexivity to consider and reconsider positions.

Teachers and others in the learning environment should model a similar reflexive attitude and should in turn communicate their past and present life questions and the way they handle them. The teacher knows his own religious biography and is aware of the influence of this biography on his present opinions, actions, and interactions with students. The teacher has knowledge of the religious development of children at different ages. Above all, the teacher is sensitive to the small and big questions which roam in the souls of students and he is capable of helping them to articulate them. Also, the teacher is sensitive to aspects of meaning attached to stories and experiences of students even when they do not speak in terms of religion or worldview. To facilitate this subjectivation of religion, the teacher is able to create a safe space in which students feel free to express what is meaningful to them.

Dialogical Responding to Plurality

Our plural society has increasing religious diversity as a feature, in which conflicting worldviews or conflicting interpretations of worldviews lead to polarization. Also, in classrooms worldview can be a source of polemics, disputes, or clashes. In view of formation toward citizenship, worldview education has the task of teaching students to look with openness at what is of ultimate value to others. Besides a reflective competence, the student therefore needs to develop a competence of receptivity of the other, who is sometimes strange. Stimulation and cultivation of basic attitudes like wonder, curiosity, and expressions of bewilderment will contribute to this competence. By allowing the strange other entrance to your heart and by experiencing openness and acknowledgment from this other, students discover themselves as humans in connectedness. This reciprocity can eventually generate a basic trust in the mystery of life. It is important that students experience religions and worldview as fields full of paradoxes, conflicts, and dilemmas which you can handle best together with others with an open and respectful attitude.

The specific task of the teacher for this aim of handling plurality in dialogue is that she recognizes and articulates differences in the classroom and that she initiates communication between the students from different backgrounds. Precisely the issues that reveal differences between students are taken as a point of engagement in a joint learning process. At these hermeneutical intersections, the teacher creates conditions for receiving information, exchanging experiences, collective investigation of sources,

Learning for Life

acquiring new experiences, a dialogical conversation, or the appropriation of new information by formulating personal reactions to the issue. Of course, the teacher must own and demonstrate the competences of receptivity, curiosity, and wonder and must model the interaction. She will instruct and train students to communicate in a terror-free manner, without exerting power over each other. In this way, students will be socialized into a democratic society.

Worldview Literacy

In worldview education, students learn gradually and dialogically what is of ultimate concern to them and to others. The answers to ultimate questions of life, provided throughout the ages, must be seen as historical, cultural, and contextual expressions. The students must get acquainted with the valuable insights about life experiences from past generations, transmitted in stories, images, symbols, views, rules, and ethical and ritual practices. Religious and nonreligious traditions and sources are a rich treasure to explore to grow in wisdom and insight. Traditions always bear the traces of the time and culture in which they originate but are at the same time changing. The students experience the relevance of these sources of wisdom for their own search for meaning and learn how others clarify their existence using traditions. It is of utmost importance that students have knowledge of the essentials of religious traditions in view of their appropriation. Worldview literacy and sensibility is no longer acquired in most of the Dutch families. To prevent the danger of religious socialization only by watching the media, which is sometimes ill-informed and often biased or one-sided, the school is preeminently the place where worldview literacy must be acquired.

Usage of religious and philosophical sources is not only a cognitive but also a spiritual process. At school, the students can experience that believing is not only a matter of the head, but above all a matter of the heart. This knowledge can be appropriated by participating in rituals or social action and by empathizing with religious stories. In the end, the student has to complete the learning process by responding to the learning experiences in an imaginative way. These answers in text, music, speech, images, etc., must be shared with the other students, and the collaborative process goes on.

The tasks of the teacher for this aim of religious literacy within the hermeneutical-communicative model is to create a free and safe space in which students can become acquainted with language, practices, and experiential qualities of religions and worldviews. The teacher has sound knowledge of the subject but also knows from his own experience what worldview can contribute and has contributed to his own life. Teachers share their experiences in a way that leaves optimal room to the students for the own attribution of meaning. As a hermeneutical specialist, the teacher points to the possibility of plural interpretations of texts and experiences and to the polyvalence of symbols and rituals. In this process of qualification, the faculties of the children regarding learning worldview will always be kept in mind.

3.2.2. Worldview Faculties of Students

Teaching can simply be described as stimulating faculties of students to let them grow. In worldview education, we would like to see that students have achieved religious competency when leaving the educational system. This means that they have a more or less coherent frame of reference of convictions, views and images about humanity and the world; that they can use this system of meaning to interpret life experiences; that they can arrange and plan their life within and from this framework; that they can communicate about their system of meaning with others.

Which faculties are especially on the agenda in worldview education? De Schepper presents six skills:

- To observe, with dimensions like wondering, feeling, enjoying, exploring.

Learning for Life

- To handle traditions, with dimensions like knowing about, knowing to connect with experience and partaking in rituals and communities.
- To imagine, with dimensions like differentiating between signs and symbols, symbolic thinking and expressing.
- To reason, with dimensions like naming, philosophizing, and valuing.
- To communicate, with dimensions like communicating with yourself and the other, changing of perspective, communicating different content (facts, experiences).
- To act, with dimensions like will, moral, making choices, daring, persevering and autonomy.[5]

These are basic faculties for all schools, public and private, to work on in worldview education. School identity can trigger an expansion of these six skills. A religious school might add "sensitization for transcendence" or "development of a hope-oriented attitude" to embody their identity.

There is no list of skills that perfectly covers the wealth of faculties that can be stimulated in education. We developed our own variant, which has some hermeneutical-communicative accents.

- Observing (looking, listening, feeling, smelling, touching).
- Wondering (being open, being curious).
- Imagining (empathizing, creating pictures, expressing, connecting to form and color).
- Telling (arranging experience in language, attributing meaning, narrating).
- Valuing (handling dilemmas, ethics, recognizing good and bad, judging, choosing).
- Reflecting (philosophizing, debating, reasoning).
- Performing a dialogue (changing perspective, listening, reacting authentically, ask questions).

5. De Schepper, *Levensbeschouwing Ontwikkelen*.

- Acting (initiating or partaking in rituals, community programs, social action).

Teachers constructing learning programs and single lessons will consciously stimulate a combination of faculties in their didactics by choosing different assignments and working methods. We find it important to consider all faculties and not act one-sidedly. There is a multiplicity of intelligence to be addressed in worldview formation. Worldview education is a holistic activity which touches upon head, heart, and hands. Discovering and attribution of meaning takes place by all these faculties. Meaning can be found in an impressive thought or line of reasoning, in participating in the Eucharist, but just as well in the experience of dark and light in Chartres Cathedral or a walk through the Rocky Mountains. Self-awareness takes place in imagining and expressing what lives within students and in the conversation about this expressions with fellow students. That conversation addresses the content of worldview education, namely the dimensions of religions and worldviews.

3.2.3. Dimensions of Worldviews

The third aspect of our hermeneutic-communicative model is the content of worldview education. The student learns to understand himself and the world in which he lives with the aid of all kinds of sources from worldviews. There is a plurality in forms of appearance as it comes to religion. We often observe a focus on dogmas, doctrines, and views in worldview education. This approach is too limited if we keep in mind that practices are very significant in religions, i.e., in Judaism or Islam. In our view, students get to know the vivid reality of worldviews in encounters in their city or village, at religious feasts or processions, in broadcasts on news networks, in documentaries, in vlogs, in reading narratives.

It is advisable to start the confrontation with religious content in the lessons by concentrating on the lived religion, as experienced and communicated by believers themselves. Lived religion is visible and recognizable for students. In addition to doctrines and philosophies, the multicolored and multifaceted practice comes to the fore. To structure this complex learning material, we use the grouping of dimensions of religion presented by religious scientist Ninian Smart.[6] We presume and have experienced that this grouping also suits nonreligious worldviews very well.

The seven dimensions (or aspects) are:

- The doctrinal and philosophical dimension (formulated ideas and concepts about man, gods, the world, creation, liberation).
- The narrative and mythic dimension (narratives, parables and legends about gods, saints, prophets, priests and sages, saviors, heroes, good and bad spirits, key moments in history).
- The ethical and legal dimension (universal principles about living a good life, laws, regulations, prescriptions, norms, values).
- The experiential and emotional dimension (emotions like awe and wonder, guilt, shame, visions, conversion, delight, ecstasy, music).
- The practical and ritual dimension (forms of expression in behavior, rituals and ceremonies, role regulation, contemplation, discipline, practice, dance).
- The social and institutional dimension (forms of organization, communities, groups, movements, institutions, leadership).
- The material dimension (architecture, art, movies, ritual objects, clothing, jewelry, holy places).

When students get acquainted with these seven aspects of religions or other worldviews, they will be stimulated in all kinds of faculties and they will grow in their worldview development. To teach religion as a differentiated and complex process, the teacher must take on four didactical roles, which form the fourth aspect of our hermeneutical-communicative model.

6. Smart, *World's Religions*, 13–21.

3.2.4. Four Didactical Roles of the Teacher

We define a didactical role as a coherent set of actions which contribute to a specific educational purpose. Pollefeyt is very brief about this subject.[7] He distinguishes three roles for worldview education teachers: the witness, the specialist, and the moderator.

In the role of the *witness*, the teacher demonstrates her involvement with her religious tradition or worldview. Teaching religion within a hermeneutical framework is not a neutral activity in which objective information is passed on. On the contrary, it is preferred that a teacher shares his views in an engaged manner, in critical dialogue with other perspectives. In this way, a teacher can function as a role model demonstrating how inhabiting a religious identity is done. Witnessing to the religion in which he is rooted or to the worldview he has adopted later in life, he mirrors a constructive way of life, leaving room for other choices and options.

The *moderator* initiates and coaches the dialogical conversations about the relationships between students' experiences and opinions and the colorful world of sources of wisdom. In this collective search for meaning, he respectfully leaves room for all kinds of identifications. The students are encouraged to construct their own religious identity and communicate that to fellow students in an open manner. The moderator offers an adequate presentation of several worldviews and religions in an open "practice room" for ideological searching, philosophizing, theologizing. He teaches the skills to handle differences respectfully.

The third role of the worldview educator is the *specialist*. While students search for meaning hermeneutically relating to sources and in a communicative way, the specialist assures that the discussed information about the different religions and worldviews is correct in view of up-to-date scientific knowledge. A lot of imaging and framing is going on in newspapers and television shows, and the teacher corrects false images and provides full and proper information. As an expert, he can not only help students to debate with proper arguments, but he can also critically evaluate

7. See Pollefeyt, *Reader Course*.

Learning for Life

truth claims of the religious traditions and other worldviews at hand. He shows them the way in the colorful world of worldviews in the seven dimensions.

In order to realize the three goals of our model, teachers must be able to take on these roles. We use a slightly different terminology better applicable to the plural and multireligious situation in the Netherlands and at the same time better suited both for public and private schools. We take *guide* for specialist, *coach* for moderator, and *role model* for witness. We add to Pollefeyt's set a fourth one: that of the *stimulator of imagination* which is crucial to fostering appropriation of religious content in the construction of identity.

A Fourth Role: Stimulator of Imagination—the Imaginator

In our view, experiencing imagination and exercising imagination are preconditions for religious learning. First, this is obvious due to the nature of the subject itself. Religions are systems of an imaginative approach to reality using narratives, mythic language, symbols, and rituals. Students must learn to understand this material in which all sort of peculiarities, impossibilities, metaphorical expressions, and symbols are present. Imagination can be seen as the power to turn absence into presence; to turn the actuality into the possible; to convert what-is into something-other-than-what is.[8] Imagination is abundantly available in religious sources. And second: in the learning process, imagination plays in a different register than cognition. It serves a different type of rationality. Roebben asserts that imagination deepens the cognitive process of seeking sense in life by penetrating spiritually into the soul of the student.[9] To understand religion, students need to develop:[10]

Metaphoric Sensitivity: The student's ability to recognize the figurative language of the narrative in words, sentences, key words,

---

8. Kearney, *Poetics of Imagining*, 4ff.
9. Roebben, *Inclusieve Godsdienstpedagogiek*, 44.
10. Berg, *Speelruimte voor Dialoog en Verbeelding*, 77–118.

and motifs, to recognize the figurative language of the narrative in existential or spiritual events and themes, and to recognize the figurative language of the narrative in the portrayal of experiences, values, and insights.

Inventive Imagination: The student's ability to make mental depictions of characters' actions and speech and of situations and themes; to emotionally conceive the otherness of characters, situations, and themes, and to create new connections between the actions and speech of characters, situations, and themes in the narrative world, and their own perceived reality.

Creative Interpretation: The student's ability to express in their own words and images the meaning of the acts and speech performed by characters in the narrative, as well as the situations and themes found in the narrative; to fill the gaps between the words and images in the narrative with their own words and images, and to find meaning and purpose in the "in-between" between the situation, themes, and characters' actions and speech found in a narrative and the student's own perceived reality.

Therefore, it is desirable to pay specific attention to this domain of imagination in didactics for worldview education. Using a neologism, we call this role the imaginator. The imaginator stimulates the students' faculty of imagination to deepen their understanding of religion and of each other.

The imaginator stimulates religious imagination and critical thinking by inviting students to respond creatively, reflexively, and interactively to symbolic/metaphorical language in stories, rituals, objects of art, architecture, and practices from religious traditions.

The four roles of coach, role model, guide, and imaginator are often connected in a lesson, in a moment of education outside the classroom, or in a ritual or service. Worldview education is a dynamic interplay of threefold hermeneutics and fourfold didactics. Depending on the subject and on the purpose of a lesson, one role or another will be at the forefront. Is a lot of sound information required (guide), or is the purpose best served by a dialogical conversation or debate (coach)? Does the subject touch on the teacher's own biography and does it offer the opportunity

Learning for Life

to share an aspect of his own spirituality (role model)? We advocate an optimal ratio of the four roles that fosters the three aims of worldview education in a balanced way. We prefer a combination of at least two of the roles in the lesson or series of lessons to distribute the faculties of the students which are triggered. Also, the role of the imaginator will preferably be used in every lesson or series of lessons to complete the educational process in an activity of appropriation. In the end, it is the construction, reconstruction, and communication of the student's worldview identity which is at stake in the collaborative and collective search for meaning in worldview education.

Worldview Faculties	Didactical Roles of the Teacher				Dimensions of Worldviews
	Guide	Coach	Role Model	Imaginator	
Observing					Doctrinal and Philosophical Dimension
Wondering					
Imagining					Narrative and Mythic Dimension
Valuing					
Telling	*Didactical Field of Dynamic Interplay of the Four Roles*				Ethical and Legal Dimension
Reflecting				
Performing a Dialog				
Acting					Experiential and Emotional Dimension
					Practical and Ritual Dimension
					Social and Institutional Dimension
					Material Dimension
Aims of Worldview Education	Personal Clarification of Existence				Aims of Worldview Education
	Dialogical Handling of Plurality				
	Worldview Literacy				

A Diagram of the Hermeneutic-Communicative Model

Learning for Life

The basis of our model is formed by the aims. For every learning moment or lesson, the worldview educator chooses which generic purpose is pursued (lowest bar in the diagram).

Subsequently, a hermeneutic-communicative learning process can be arranged via several possible trajectories:

- The teacher can start with an experience, question, or story posed by a student and think of what worldview faculty she would like to stimulate (first column). Then she can consider the content and turn to the dimensions of worldview and choose one of them which serves the subject best (last column). And then she decides which didactic role she would like to take to stimulate adequate learning (middle columns).

- Another trajectory may go like this: starting point is again an experience, question, or story posed by a student; then there may be a philosophical or religious dimension that fits very well for this starting point (last column); next the teacher chooses which faculty could be stimulated to grow and best suits the chosen source (first column). Then the teacher decides which role to take (middle columns).

- Of course, there could be reasons to start with a religious dimension, for example because a religious festival or feast is coming up in the next few days or weeks, maybe Easter. The teacher wants to explore the biblical narratives of Easter to work on the generic purpose of religious literacy. He will then think about the life experiences of the students who are, or may be associated with, for example, experiences of new life in nature, in the family, or in the rabbit cage at home. He then chooses a religious faculty, for example telling, and finally chooses the didactical role, for example the guide.

The teacher varies between all the aspects of the model, while always focusing on the three generic goals and balancing the didactical roles. We give some examples.

- A conversation takes place on the school playground between children about the burqini worn by Muslim women and whether they should be banned. This prompts the teacher of group 7 (age ten/eleven) to start a learning process. The teacher wants to start working on the generic purpose of worldview literacy; she chooses the ethical or legal dimension from the column of worldview dimensions (last column) and takes examples from Islamic law as the subject matter; she wants to stimulate the faculty of reflecting (first column) and it seems to her best suited to take the role of guide; she wants to explain how laws work in Islam, where the principles come from in time and in cultural contexts and so on. From this line of thinking, she develops working methods and materials.

- A student tells about a sick grandmother and wonders whether God can really heal people. The teacher sees an opportunity to work on these questions within the generic aim of clarifying personal existence; he notes that he feels drawn to take a witness role because he wants to show how he deals with this theme in his life (role model); he chooses to stimulate the faculty of imagining so that students can process this vulnerable theme individually (first column); finally, he chooses the experiential and emotional dimension from the worldview sources; from Christianity he chooses some texts from the book of Psalms.

These choices provide a framework for the practical arrangement of the learning moment. In choosing the didactic role, the teacher will always realize that these roles serve the learning process. This will often be the last step in the thought process in preparation for a lesson. First, we have to establish aims, dimensions, faculties, and then the didactic role or roles that best support that route can be picked.

Learning for Life

To picture the process:

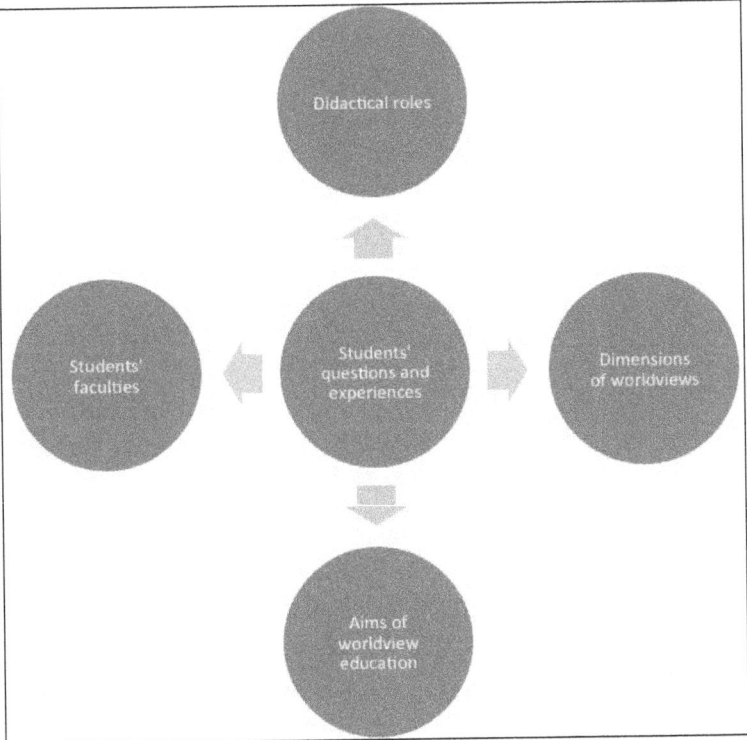

Figure 2. Picture of the Hermeneutiscal-Communicatieve Teaching Process

There are infinite possibilities to design learning trajectories.

Chapter 4

Staging Dialogical Worldview Education

Research Outcomes

IN THIS CHAPTER WE show how our hermeneutical-communicative model was implemented and contextualized in the practices of nine schools in a two-year action research project. (4.1) Then we look at the nine schools to get a picture of the results in the three regions in the Netherlands (4.2). We conclude with a meta-analysis based on the reports of the participating teachers (4.3) and an evaluation (4.4).

4.1. PRACTICE DEVELOPMENT AND RESEARCH

Does the model work? First, we must clarify what we mean by "work" in this context. Many people have an impression of research as an activity in which a distant researcher collects and analyzes data to say something about reality. There is a practice that develops, and there is the researcher. The researcher looks through a microscope, explains what he or she observes, says something about cause and effect, and tries to make predictions

Staging Dialogical Worldview Education

about the future. An example would be the introduction of a new calculation method: a practice book is devised based on a number of theoretical insights and design assumptions, it is introduced at several schools, and the researchers measure the extent to which the learning achievements of the students improve objectively after the introduction of the new method. *Learning for Life* is a research project of a different kind. There is no distant researcher who acted from a private position to design interventions which would be implemented by others, after which the researcher estimates what the results are. *Learning for Life* is a practice development project, in which questions and solutions of teachers themselves take center stage and are leading in the research process. As scholars at Marnix University and Windesheim University, we were no distant observers; rather, we were very engaged with the questions and possible solutions of the teachers. Practice development and research went hand in hand. The developers of the practice were also at the same time researchers of their own practice. This form of development and research is considered action research. The methodology that we have used is the Professional Learning Community, abbreviated to PLC. PLCs are sometimes called practice development groups, for instance in the context of health care. What works is defined and owned by the practitioners in these PLCs themselves.

PLCs

There are all kinds of PLCs in educational contexts, and several definitions are in use. The term has become a fuzzy concept.[1] There is some common ground, of course. In our case, a PLC is a research community of teachers, teacher trainees and tutors/researchers from our universities. PLCs have a few starting points:

(1) We use the professional expertise of the participants in the PLC. Their skills, their knowledge, their experience, their

---

1. Lomos et al., *Professional Communities*.

vision, and their creativity are ingredients of a fruitful development process.

(2) In order to improve actual practice, the appropriate innovations should start within the same practice. A PLC works well when professionals identify problems to be solved and when research starts with their definition of the situation. Their experiences, ideas, and tacit knowledge point out directions as to where solutions should be sought. Theory follows practice and it should not be the other way around.

(3) The PLC leaders (and possibly also students from the universities involved) provide theoretical input to the PLC. In this way, the intended interaction between theory and practice takes place. In our case, this was the hermeneutical-communicative model of worldview education.

A definition of PLCs could be formulated as follows:

> Teachers form part of a professional community when they share a common view on the school's mission, mutually reflect on instructional practices, cooperate, engage in reflective dialogue, and provide one another with feedback on teaching activities, all with a focus on student learning.[2]

In the same article, Lomos et al. describe five interacting characteristics of effective professional learning communities:

- Reflective dialogue: discuss teachers' educational themes with each other.

- Shared autonomy in practice (deprivatization of practice): teachers visit each other's classes and give each other feedback.

- Cooperation: teachers working together in different ways.

- Shared lived objectives (shared sense of purpose): teachers share the mission of the school.

- Collective focus on students and their learning process: teachers feel jointly responsible for what and how the students learn.

2. Lomos et al., *Professional Communities*, 120–21.

Staging Dialogical Worldview Education

Reflection and cooperation are the key words. The objective of the PLCs we have arranged was to jointly create new teaching methods and new curricula from the perspective of our hermeneutical-communicative model.

In the first year teachers developed new practices, appropriating the hermeneutical-communicative model to their own context in lessons, parts of lessons, in rituals and projects. In the second year the teachers and teams of teachers constructed chains of lessons and year programs from the perspective of the model.

4.2. PORTRAITS OF NINE LEARNING FOR LIFE SCHOOLS

In this section, nine schools that participated in *Leren voor het Leven (Learning for Life*, 2014–2016) will be portrayed. Furthermore, new practices of student-centered, dialogical worldview education will be elaborated upon. To do so, we take peeks into the existing practices in the northern region of the Netherlands (*Regio Noord*) at schools around Zwolle, in the middle region (*Regio Midden*) at schools around Utrecht, and in the southern region (*Regio Zuid*) at schools in the province of Zeeland.

4.2.1. The Northern Region of the Netherlands

We start this chapter by discussing the personal motives of a teacher called "N." at De Zevensprong, a primary school in Dronten. We learn about a new practice for worldview education at this school. Then, we will outline several lessons taught around the holiday of Pentecost at De Es, a primary school in Hellendoorn. Lastly, we will describe the research worldview questions at De Carrousel primary school in Dalfsen.

Learning for Life

Primary School De Zevensprong in Dronten

Dronten is home to the Protestant Christian primary school De Zevensprong. The school uses a worldview teaching method called *Kind op Maandag* (Child on Monday). N., a teacher-in-training, and L., a full-time teacher, are involved in the *Learning for Life* project. Aside from their participation, the two teachers passionately put effort into inspiring enthusiasm in the rest of their team for a new practice of worldview education in which biblical narratives and the students' own worldview questions are discussed thematically.

Personal Motives

N. has been working at De Zevensprong for fourteen years. During those years, she taught worldview education in the same way: each morning, she read a passage from a biblical narrative from the method *Kind op Maandag* to her students. Then, she would ask the students to reproduce what had just been read to them: "What happened to Moses?" Typically, only one or two of the students would respond. The allotted time would pass, the students had received the required dose of biblical narratives, and arithmetic could now begin. This procedure would occur five days per week.

N. had been developing her own beliefs for quite a while. Over the years, she started looking at the Bible from a new perspective. She could no longer see the narratives as having actually happened. She increasingly struggled with the question of how to explain the biblical narratives to the students. Worldview questions such as "If God created the earth, what did Allah do?" were dismissed. When a student asked, "Is the story of Genesis true?" she would respond: "Yes, it is."

During the PLC (Professional Learning Community) session, N. learns that she wants to tell the children what she believes, what she really thinks is important. N. says: "Surely I can't tell them that God created the world in seven days? But I can say that I think that it's extraordinary that there's a sun, that there's a moon. That

Staging Dialogical Worldview Education

it becomes dark and then light again. To me, that has to signify a higher power." Furthermore, she wants to share her personal life and motives with her students. She passionately tells the story of an Afghan family that regularly joins her family for dinner. How curious her children are about the turban worn by the father of the Sikh family and about their sacred texts. And then comes the revelation: "They have the same values. Love, forgiveness, sharing, peace." N. clearly knows what she wants. She wants to "do it differently, to let the students familiarize themselves with diversity in the broadest sense of the word."

Slowly but surely, N. transforms her worldview education lessons. She is no longer a "witness"; she is now a "role model" (which is one of the four roles a teacher can adopt in our approach to worldview education). She says: "I'm 'evangelizing' a lot less and instead I show the students what religion means to me without the intention to tell them what *the* truth is." N. can now be herself and share her own beliefs, her own motivations, and her own passions with the children.

Learned a Lot

N. has learned a lot. Hermeneutical communication now has a central role in the worldview education lessons. She consciously adopts different teaching roles and pays attention to the students' own realities and experiences. By offering a variety of didactic formats, she teaches students to wonder at the sources offered, which in turn become meaningful. The students now conduct real dialogues with one another. By pairing the students up in the guiding conversations, they learn to formulate their thoughts, to listen to each other and to understand each other. Apart from that, the students collaborate in small groups; together, they make drawings, collages, small plays, or word webs. Lastly, N.'s flow has inspired L. (a colleague) to do the same.

Learning for Life

Teaching Format

Through their efforts, the two teachers have caused change within the rest of their team. For example, the team abandoned the method *Kind op Maandag*. Instead, N. and L. developed a new teaching format which is divided into monthly themes based on biblical narratives and worldview questions. They emphasize finding meaning, primarily in biblical narratives, for instance through addressing the students' worldview questions, but also during the monthly celebrations. During these celebrations, each class presents the meanings they find in the worldview education lessons in their own way.

Furthermore, the teachers say they aim to generate more attention for the focal point of hermeneutic communication: learning to deal with diversity.[3] Both teachers already do so in their lessons. For example, L. devotes more time and attention to students that have a different religious background than before. Based on their own contexts, the students tell their classmates about their own worldviews. For instance, a Jewish boy explained why he wears a yarmulke, and a Moroccan boy showed how to perform an Islamic prayer. Furthermore, the teachers aim to invite representatives of various religions to their courses on worldview education in future.

Results of Learning for Life

As a result of the project, the practice of reading biblical narratives from *Kind op Maandag* to the class and asking the children to simply reproduce elements from those readings evolved into a school-wide worldview project in which hermeneutical communication has a central role. The school aims to accomplish this by using biblical narratives. What follows is an example of a teaching format that spans one year. The sources used in the teaching format for the younger groups include the *Samenleesbijbel* (The Bible to Read Together, a version in plainer language) and a Bible with

3. Cf. chapter 2.

Staging Dialogical Worldview Education

pictures. Both smaller and larger worldview questions raised by the children are the focal point:[4]

Year 1: September	Groups 1–2	Groups 3–4	Groups 5–6	Groups 7–8
Creation Stewardship Worldview Steps 1–3 route 2 (pp. 25–29)	Creation 1. The first people	On which days did God create humankind? The meaning of the seventh day. How did God create humankind? What does God look like? Where is God?	Stewardship How do you interact with nature? How do you interact with animals? How do people interact with animals in the Bible?	Creation of Earth How do you feel about the creation of Earth? What do you think of the big bang?
Good and Evil Steps 4–6 route 2 (pp. 30–37)	Adam and Eve and the Tree of Knowledge of Good and Evil	Good and Evil What is good and what is evil?	Theme page 16: Animals (p. 78) What do you believe is good and what is evil? How do you deal with these concepts?	Why is there so much suffering in the world?
Promise Steps 1–5 route 3 (pp. 38–48)	Noah 2. A year spent on the water	What is the meaning of the rainbow?	Promises should be kept.	What does a promise mean to us in modern times?
Language Step 6 route 3 (pp. 48–50)	The Tower of Babel 12. The highest tower		Foreign languages (p. 49)	

4. These are Bibles that are used at many primary schools.

Learning for Life

Primary School De Es in Hellendoorn

The Protestant Christian primary school De Es is situated in Hellendoorn. Its principal, R., participated in the project, as did teachers H. and M. and teacher-in-training N. Their worldview lessons consist primarily of reading a biblical narrative to the students and asking them to reproduce what occurred in the narrative afterward. The participants have been searching for a new method for worldview education in which they can centralize religious holidays from various traditions, biblical narratives and the students' worldview questions.

The Meaning of Pentecost to Children

Almost no one knows what Pentecost means, even though the story is read to the class every year. —K., a sixth-year student

Teacher-in-training N. has conducted a survey regarding the students' satisfaction, which showed that most students did not find the worldview education lessons interesting and that they felt they learned only a little. To N., it was clear: "Children cannot find meaning in the reading of biblical narratives to the class and the subsequent demand of reproducing what had happened in the narrative." She decided to introduce change: to let the lessons revolve around the students' own experiences. For the *Learning for Life* project, R., H., and N. herself developed a teaching format that addresses holidays from various religious traditions, biblical narratives and worldview questions raised by the students.

During the last PLC meeting, N. shows how a set of lessons revolving around Pentecost was made meaningful for sixth-year students. Two of these students are present as well. They say: "The worldview education lessons were boring. You couldn't do anything on your own and you forgot what the story was about." As a result, the goal for the new set of lesson plans is as follows: "Pentecost has to become meaningful for *all* children." N. emphasizes the diversity in the groups: "The days off on Pentecost Holidays

Staging Dialogical Worldview Education

are spent in various ways: one child attends church, while another goes to the mall."

The Pentecost tradition is a narrative of hope, passion, fire, and enthusiasm. These themes are close to the students' own realities. Through the use of such phrases, the participants hope to entice the students to think about the themes of the holiday. N., R., and H. subsequently decide to introduce several new didactic formats in which they appeal to the worldview capabilities of the students. Furthermore, they consciously employ varying teaching roles. The aim is to spark the students' curiosities for the tradition of Pentecost and to get them to think about it, to imagine it, for themselves.

Pentecost Lessons

N. starts the first lesson by having the group study an image of the biblical narrative of Pentecost. She asks the students what they see and which thoughts and feelings the image provokes. One child sees a man who prays, while another sees a man who consoles another person. The students' thoughts revolve around love, warmth, hope, and "healing hands."

During the second lesson, a teacher-in-training tells the narrative. The children listen breathlessly. Afterward, the teacher-in-training shows the students a video clip in which the Pentecost narrative is told humorously in a minute and a half. This sparks a discussion. Some children believe the story is too straightforward or too funny. N. says: "Some students suddenly wanted to show that they think the Pentecost narrative is important."

During the third lesson, the teacher-in-training has the class discuss the Holy Spirit. She conducts a worldview dialogue with the students. She asks them about their fires, their passions, about what drives them and about their hopes for themselves, their families, their friends, and the world as a whole. Then, she asks them to describe what their own Holy Spirit looks like and what it means to them. In small groups, the students draw pictures of their own Holy Spirits in a variety of creative ways. What follows are presentations of these drawings. Gusts of wind, fires, queens, hands, and rainbows all come into play. Meaningful words such as "protection," "colorful," "inspiration," "untouchable," and "healing hands" are mentioned.

Goal Achieved

After these lessons, all sixth-year students have attributed a personal meaning to Pentecost, as well as a meaning they themselves found in the tradition. N., R., and H. have achieved their goal and the children responded positively. K., the boy whose quote is shown above, says: "The Pentecost lessons are fun now, because we get to think for ourselves, we can express our opinions, and we do not have to agree with one another. I know what Pentecost is now."

Results of Learning for Life

The result of the *Learning for Life* project at De Es was the evolution from a teaching method in which a biblical narrative was read to the students, after which they were asked to reproduce what had taken place, to a school-wide project regarding worldview education in which hermeneutic communication was a central focus. The school chooses to do so by using the holidays of various religions, biblical narratives, and the students' own worldview questions. Below, we show two concrete results of the project conducted at De Es in Hellendoorn.

The first is a table showing a framework for worldview education when it comes to competences. Then there is a concrete delineation of the curriculum for March 2017, in which the relation to the students' social and emotional development is outlined. The students' worldview questions in this learning process are connected to the religious holidays throughout.

Staging Dialogical Worldview Education

Groups 1-2	Groups 3-4	Groups 5-6	Groups 7-8
Emphasis on familiarization (Perception, experiencing, familiarizing)	Emphasis on familiarization (Perception, experiencing, familiarizing, meeting)	Emphasis on learning how it works, recognizing cohesion and insight (Applying insights)	Emphasis on correlations, interpretation, dilemmas (Attitudes, applying insights)
Hears biblical narratives and learns to respond to them	Hears biblical narratives and learns to respond to them		
	Encounters worldview questions and learns to ask them	Knows how to ask worldview questions, how to talk about them and how to explore them	Knows worldview questions, can identify dilemmas
Encounters holidays and experiences them	Encounters holidays and experiences them	Can identify the connection between worldview questions, holidays and religions	Can identify several dilemmas surrounding holidays and religions and can provide arguments and perspectives

Framework

Learning for Life

Celebration	Worldview Question	Social Development	Worldview	Group
Day of Prayer	What is space?	Where do you live? What aspects of nature do you enjoy? Are you happy where you live? Where would you like to go?	Do you feel responsible for the earth? What do you to make the space around you comfortable? Did God create the earth consciously or was its creation a coincidence?	1–8
Easter	What are the meanings of happiness and life, but also of suffering and death?	When are you happy and when are you sad? Who do you go to when you are happy and when you are sad? Who are your real friends, who you can go to with both happiness and sadness? Are you part of the group or are you an outsider? Do you feel like you belong/can be yourself?	What are the meanings of happiness and life? What are the meanings of suffering and death? Why do people die? Can God console you at certain times? Do you prefer talking about happiness and life over talking about suffering and death? What do you think you could change about this? What would you want to change?	5–8

Teaching Plan, March 2017

De Carrousel in Dalfsen

Primary school De Carrousel is a public school situated in Dalfsen. For years now, the school has offered optional lessons in religious education and humanistic education to its students. Principal A., teacher M., and teacher-in-training G. are passionately involved in the project. They want to innovate the way in which worldview education is taught at their school in such a way that it is in line with the multicultural Dutch society of 2016.

Staging Dialogical Worldview Education

Letting Go of Old Formats

Public primary school De Carrousel let go of the old format in which the lessons for worldview education were dictated by the teacher who was hired to teach. In their new view regarding worldview education, the lessons are supposed to revolve around the students. The aim of the school is to not be passively neutral, but rather to be actively pluriform when it comes to worldview. The first reason for M. to participate in our project was to explore how a religious holiday (like Pentecost) can be taught at a public primary school. The school aims to achieve its openness by means of actively offering religious education, because of its cultural and societal relevance. During the first year of the project, M. conducted research and wrote a document outlining a vision for religious education at a public school. During the second year, A., M., and G. designed an interesting set of lessons for the older groups: a research project in which the students' worldview questions are the core.

Preparation and Framework: Researching Worldview Questions

In preparation for the research project, principal A. explained to a group of seventh- and eighth-year students that there are small and large worldview questions. He invited the students to write down their own worldview questions. He was surprised (and touched) to see that this resulted in many different questions, such as: "Why are refugees sent back if they arrive only barely alive?"; "Why do refugees suffer if there is a God?"; and "What does freedom mean for future development?" In cooperation with the students, A. categorized these questions into several themes, such as: the right to exist, citizenship, religion, and politics.

The goal of the research project is to familiarize students with the various religious movements which play an important role in the Dutch multicultural society and to teach them to deal with people's differing beliefs respectfully. Teacher-in-training G.

enthusiastically recalls the research project. It started with a very recent theme: freedom. He lets the children listen to the Dutch song *Vrijheid* (Freedom) by Jeroen Schippers. Then, he guides the students in a worldview dialogue. He asks questions such as: "Who is the 'I' in the song?" and "Who are you?" As a result, the students are more aware of the diversity within their group. They not only list differences in appearance, age, and family structure, but also differences in religious and moral beliefs.

G. asks the students which worldview questions they think of when they hear the word "freedom." In small groups, they discuss this topic and formulate questions such as: "Why are refugees sent home after they have just arrived?"; "If there is a God?"; "Why do refugees suffer?"; and "What does freedom entail for my development?" Per group, the students choose which question they find most important, most beautiful, or most powerful. The teacher-in-training then helps them formulate sub-questions that fit their worldview question.

G. explains that the students keep a checklist in which the hermeneutical-communicative model is outlined. The sub-questions should address key components contained within this model, such as diversity and rituals.

The Method Chosen by a Group of Students

An example of a worldview question chosen by one group of students is: "Why are there refugees in the world?" They formulate sub-questions such as: "How many refugees are there in the world?"; "Which countries accept refugees?"; and "How do Judaism, Christianity, and Islam regard refugees?" They then consult books and the internet to answer these questions. They discover that there are different kinds of refugees, that refugees come from various countries, and that there are various reasons for becoming a refugee. They also discover that the different Abrahamic religions regard refugees in similar ways: the Torah, the Bible, and the Quran all contain stories about refugees, such as the Jewish people

Staging Dialogical Worldview Education

fleeing Egypt to the promised land of Israel, or Muhammad and his followers fleeing from Mecca to Medina.

On the internet, the students come across a video clip of a refugee family. The children flee by train, but the parents cannot join them. The students also come across photographs of shelters for Syrian refugees: families on the run because their lives are in danger, photos of small children playing in tents.

They can then process the information they found in various ways. They get the opportunity to give a presentation using PowerPoint, Prezi, a poster, a visual design, or a play. During these presentations, both the result as well as the process are discussed; they not only discuss what is learned in terms of content, but also in terms of the way in which their exploration took place. Were the students' worldview questions answered? Has their view of the world changed? Did the research raise new questions for the students? G. believes that using the hermeneutical model to ponder and discuss these questions with the students will indeed develop the students' worldviews.

A New View on Worldview Education

Through the research, a new view on worldview education is clearly coming to fruition, a view which fits the multireligious Dutch society in 2016 and in which the student has a central role. The primary role of the teacher is to offer guidance, to be a role model, and to provide stimuli. The student owns his or her own learning process. There is room to discover meaning. The students formulate their own worldview questions that correspond to current events, learn to think about these questions critically, and find answers in various sources, for instance religious sources. G. expresses a desire to "pay even more attention to diversity by inviting representatives from various religions to class."

Results of Learning for Life

The result of *Learning for Life* at De Carrousel is the evolution from a teacher-guided, autonomous model of worldview education into a school-wide worldview project in which hermeneutical communication is a central focus. The school chooses to realize this by having older primary school groups investigate the worldview questions formulated by the students. It is a first step toward a new model for worldview education. A new educational framework is being developed.

4.2.2. Middle Region of the Netherlands

In the middle region of the country, three more primary schools participated in the two-year project *Learning for Life*: Catholic primary school De Achtbaan and Protestant Christian primary school De Parkschool, both situated in Utrecht, and primary school De Horn in Wijk bij Duurstede. All three schools spent two years developing new practices for meaningful worldview education within the context of their own school in collaboration with one another, with students, with researchers and with teacher training advisers. The following report shows the results of this project for each of the three schools.

De Achtbaan, Utrecht

It is Monday morning. As usual, the fifth-year students watch the children's daily news (*Het Jeugdjournaal*) during their lunch break. Based on this short, age-appropriate news show, the topic of conversation is confidence. The teacher asks, "What is confidence?" Siebren responds: "That you trust yourself." The teacher says, "Well done, Siebren. Does anyone have anything to add to this?" "That you know you can do it," Anne says. Then the class falls silent. The teacher thinks intensely; how can she delve further into this subject? There has to be more that can be said. "Who can think of a situation in which they had no confidence?" Ibe raises his hand

Staging Dialogical Worldview Education

and, after the teacher calls on him, says: "When I had to take the swimming test for my C diploma, I didn't know if I would pass." The teacher asks: "And how did you feel?" Ibe responds: "My stomach hurt a little." The teacher says: "And would it have hurt less if you had talked about it with someone?" Ibe nods. The bell rings. The students can now go outside to play. The teacher remains in the classroom and contemplates: "Why can't I let more children speak? Why do I find it difficult to delve deeper into certain subjects? Which questions would allow me to do so?"

During the lunch break, she consults the internal counsellor. She explains the situation and asks if the counsellor knows how she can increase the profundity of the conversations to get the students to think more deeply. The counsellor takes a fan from her drawer. "Look," she says, "I think this BLOOM tool might prove very useful." The teacher studies the guide that comes with the BLOOM tool so that she can prepare better for her lessons for the following day.

The situation described above will surely sound familiar to many teachers. This is particularly likely in the following sense: how does one conduct a meaningful and productive dialogue involving the entire class? The teacher could simply ask the same questions of each individual student and hear various examples stemming from the students' own realities, but to do more than just gathering experiences or images often proves difficult. Courses revolving around social skills are often taught in the same set ways and rarely achieve the goal the teacher had intended. After all, how often do you feel that the students are truly (or rather: deeply) learning? How do you know you are achieving your goals? Is it good practice to adhere to a certain method?

With these questions in mind, teachers from the primary school De Achtbaan in Utrecht collaborated with a Marnix Academy research group on *Dynamische Identiteitsontwikkeling* (Dynamic Identity Development) and a fourth-year academic student learning to become a teacher. They developed a "BLOOM tool": a paper fan which teachers can use to shape their teaching in such a way that critical thinking occurs in their classes.

75

Learning for Life

Bloom's Taxonomy (2001)

Bloom's taxonomy was published in 1956 by American educational psychologist Benjamin Bloom. Originally developed for history lessons, it was slightly altered over the years; to this day, it still offers a useful framework for describing learning processes. Bloom believes that people understand things on several levels. The skills that relate to this are organized in levels of increasing difficulty. Each new level of understanding is more complicated and always incorporates the previous. Before we can understand something, we need to remember it; before we can apply it, we must understand it, and so on. Bloom's initial mapping of this was revised by Anderson in 2001, who replaced the nouns by verbs to underline the notion that activity is a prerequisite for improvement.

The fan (the BLOOM tool) is a practical instrument that offers questions the teacher can ask to induce critical thinking at each level of difficulty. The questions included in it are the result of teachers studying various sources. These include sources stemming from developmental psychology, sources stemming from worldview methods of learning, and sources on twenty-first-century learning. The reasoning behind its name is that Bloom's taxonomy turned out to be very important in the development of the tool. It is interesting to note that the tool was developed with the various primary school levels in mind. As a result, it offers different questions for the upper and lower age groups at the primary school level.

The Process

The research question, then, was as follows: "How can we enhance the critical thinking of our students?" Based on a literature review, the research project was set in motion. In particular, research into "asking the right questions" led to eye-opening insights. The decision was made not only to seek an answer to the question asked by the teacher, but to develop a tool which helps teachers ask the right questions in their class to get the students to think critically: the

Staging Dialogical Worldview Education

BLOOM tool. These questions are also known as "higher-order thinking" questions. Through a lot of practice and further rehearsal of Bloom's theory and taxonomy, the well-thought-out and remarkably useful tool was eventually developed. The starting point was the revised taxonomy of Bloom, by Anderson and Kratwohl (2001).

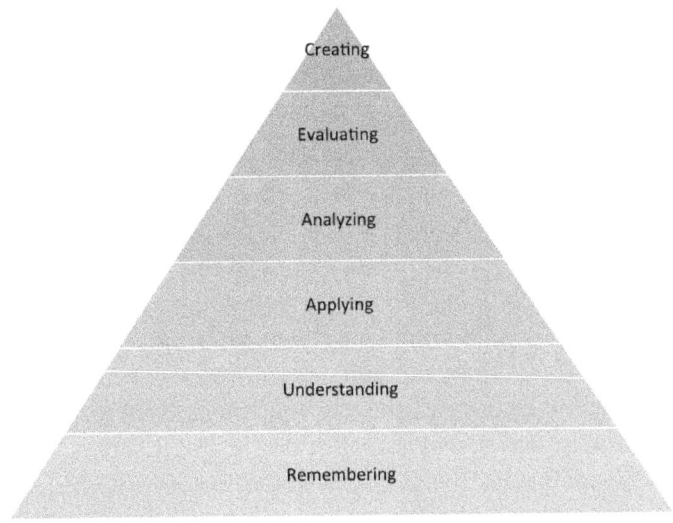

Figure 3. Revised Taxonomy of Bloom (Anderson and Kratwohl, 2001)

In practice, it turned out that students appreciate these sorts of questions; they appreciate being allowed time to think, and the fact that there is no right or wrong answer. When asked if they needed to think "harder" when asked these questions, one student responded: "Yes, because there isn't always a right answer." Another interesting quote was the result of the following question: "Is this also important to learn?" The student's response: "Yes, because you also have to learn things other than spelling and arithmetic."

Another strength of the BLOOM tool is the fact that the teacher, when he or she discovers which way of asking questions leads to more critical thinking, can employ that same method for different subjects.

Learning for Life

Results of Learning for Life

Some of the characteristics of twenty-first-century education are critical thinking and asking questions.[5] Critical thinking and asking the right questions is something that was hardly employed at De Achtbaan, which resulted in the decision to employ these characteristics. Teachers from the primary school De Achtbaan in Utrecht collaborated with the research program *Dynamische Identiteitsontwikkeling* (Dynamic Identity Development) and a fourth-year academic student learning to become a teacher. They developed in cooperation a "BLOOM tool": a paper fan which teachers can use to shape their teaching in such a way that critical thinking occurs in their classes. The fan (the BLOOM tool) is a practical instrument that offers questions the teacher can ask to induce critical thinking at each level of difficulty. The questions included in it are the result of teachers studying various sources. These include sources stemming from developmental psychology, sources stemming from worldview methods of learning and sources on twenty-first-century learning. A specific strength of the BLOOM tool is that the teacher who has discovered which questions lead to more critical thinking, can employ that same method for different subjects.

De Horn in Wijk bij Duurstede

Primary school De Horn is a public primary school situated in Wijk bij Duurstede and is attended by around 250 students. In line with its public nature, it is accessible to all. Its aim is to offer a safe, familiar, and engaged pedagogical climate to its students in which tolerance and solidarity are key. These notions are explicitly foregrounded in its curriculum by way of the lessons on "social development," but the school also aims to set a good example for its students. The school considers it its duty to contribute pedagogically to the students' development into autonomous, competent, and socially competent people. In doing so, the uniqueness

---

5. Platform Onderwijs 2032. *Ons Onderwijs2032*.

Staging Dialogical Worldview Education

of each student is acknowledged and considered to be a positive aspect rather than a problem. Where possible, the school attempts to respond to each individual student's capabilities, interests, and needs. In their curriculum, they strive for broad and uninterrupted development of the students within a neatly outlined structure.

This broad development is made visible through the attention they pay to the cognitive, affective, and creative development of the student and the balance they seek between the transfer of knowledge and the development of (strategic) skills. They want students to learn to deal with the world around them and to learn to utilize the opportunities they are given: "The Netherlands within the world, the world within the Netherlands"; at De Horn, internationalization is an important part of the curriculum. Starting from this context and vision, teachers at De Horn discovered that, as a result of the existing results-oriented approach, they were left with little time and opportunity for the students to "meet" one another in class. By "meeting," they mean that the students get to listen to one another, see one another, and appreciate one another within the confines of the classroom. Lessons were designed in such a way that results took precedence over all else. There was hardly any room for slower questions, which conflicted with the school's vision.

The Process

The teachers at De Horn needed some time to get used to the delineation of ambitions within the joint process of *Learning for Life*. If possible, they would have preferred to see the path they had to take in advance, with clear goals made visible. In other words, thinking rationally still took precedence over passion. Slowly but surely, through employing teaching methods which appealed to the heart, their ambitions became clear to themselves. They did, however, demand that it should not be an addition to their workload, asking for it to be a tool that would allow them to connect their lessons with others and which would be applicable across the board.

Learning for Life

After the first two meetings with teachers from other schools, it soon became clear that the term *dialogizing* suited De Horn. The teachers read literature from various perspectives regarding this subject; they considered it from a pedagogical standpoint, but also from the perspectives of developmental psychology and worldview. Eventually, they could envision what was feasible in each age category at their school when it came to the development of the worldview capabilities of their students. Learning to appreciate themselves and others was key in that sense.

The Teachers' Perspective: What Was Class Like?

The class was taught based on a lesson from *Nieuwsbegrip*, a Dutch online source which offers interactive lessons for reading comprehension, arithmetic, and spelling, in which the discovery of a new planet was discussed. The video clip incorporated in this lesson had already been seen by the students before, which ensured they had some preexisting knowledge. During the lesson, more in-depth questions were asked to spark the curiosity of the students.

The teacher briefly referenced the previous lesson, after which he or she introduced the main question of the current lesson: "What else do you think we will explore in space? What would it be like in thirty years?" The students were then given some time to think, after which they got to individually write down their thoughts regarding the main question on a piece of paper. After that time had passed, the students got to share their thoughts in pairs, an activating work format. In this work format, they paid close attention to whoever was speaking and did not stray from the subject.

When the students had finished discussing their findings, the teacher initiated a class-wide conversation. During this conversation, the teachers alternated between asking open and closed questions. Closed questions were mostly asked as a follow-up, an example of which is the following: "Would it be a similar life form to the ones we know?" The teacher's attitude was generally fairly restrained, giving the students the opportunity to respond to each

Staging Dialogical Worldview Education

other. The students appeared to know how to do so; they took turns without raising their hands and only one student spoke at a time. The rest would look at the student who was speaking. Initially, it tended to be the same students who spoke up. The teacher would then try to involve more students: A certain student says this. "What do you think about that, [other student]?" In this way, other students were challenged to voice their opinion. Later on, many different students spoke in the conversation. And although the students were able to respond to one another freely, the teacher did ensure that other students got to take a turn as well. While doing so, the teacher would combine the opinions of several students, for example by saying: "What I hear you guys say now is that . . ." During the class-wide conversation, the students appeared to respect the expressions or opinions of others. An example of this is one student's reaction to another student's remark: "You can say that again!" They also justified and backed up the statements they made. An example of this is the fact that the students would refer to the video clip they had watched, which helped them come to their conclusion as a result of a series of logical steps. The teacher then ended the lesson by briefly summarizing which conclusions the class had drawn, after which she told them that she thought it was a nice conversation and thanked the students. During this lesson several worldview skills were developed.

Results of Learning for Life

Thanks to the *Learning for Life* project, the teachers saw the opportunity to fine-tune their lessons to be more in line with the goals they had set. They took on the challenge of paying more attention to the students "meeting" one another and set out to find a method which could be employed in all age categories. As a result, they did not have to teach an additional subject, but instead found a way to connect several others. The teachers set out to design lessons in which dialogue played a central role. The first step was reading comprehension, the second emotional development; eventually, they arrived at art and worldview education. This last subject became their final design for an educational framework, which was to be rolled out across the entire school in 2017.

Two important subjects for this lesson were dialogizing pertaining to a certain subject and wondering about a subject.

In the middle age groups, dialogizing consists of being able to conduct a dialogue together, during which the students learn to let each other finish and accept that others have opinions that differ from their own. In this particular conversation, the students managed to both let each other finish and voice their own opinions very well. At times, the level of sophistication during the conversation was raised to a higher age level because the students responded to the expressions of others. A possible next step could be to challenge the students to question one another when it comes to their expressions and opinion, during which one student attempts to empathize with another. At the level of the middle age groups, wondering encapsulates the development of curiosity pertaining to subjects originating from their own environment or from art, culture, or simple current societal matters. During this lesson, the students developed curiosity about one current event more than any other: the discovery of a new planet. They were challenged to connect this event to their own curiosity and imagination.

De Parkschool in Utrecht

Historically, De Parkschool is a Protestant Christian primary school situated in Lombok in the city of Utrecht. Most of its students (70%) come from an Islamic background. Also, Christians, Hindus, and nonreligious students attend the school. They describe themselves as a multicultural school and they believe it is important that each student at their school is heard, respected, and given the chance to practice their own beliefs while also learning about other religious traditions. To properly shape their worldview education, the school has decided to participate in *Learning for Life*.

Staging Dialogical Worldview Education

Teaching Methods

The students have been actively engaged in the subjects through the use of various teaching methods. For instance, the project week was opened by way of a school-wide introduction: several upper-level students gave a presentation on their findings from the internet about Holi. Afterward, several kindergartners performed a spring dance which fit in with the theme of Holi: a new beginning. Over the following days, each teacher gave three lessons on Holi. The subject matter consisted of the Holi narratives (which was adapted to be in line with the groups' levels), which were supported by a "class chest" which contained further narrative content (for instance, objects that featured in the narrative could be found in the chests). The goal of the lesson was to transfer knowledge and to increase the students' involvement. During the second lesson, the children were asked which aspect of the narrative had had the largest impact on them. They then got to show this by way of a creative assignment. They were given the opportunity to choose for themselves which materials they would use. Drawings, clay figurines, and paintings which all showed different aspects of the holiday of Holi were made and handed in. During the third lesson, worldview questions surrounding Holi were the central focus. The teacher would initiate the lesson by asking a question (e.g., "What would it be like to start all over?") and the students were given the opportunity to express their thoughts, which resulted in follow-up questions. Participation by the students played a primary role. To close the themed week, the children were tasked with writing down a negative thought or bad dream on a piece of paper, which they then tossed into a brazier placed on the playground, symbolically leaving these negative experiences behind. The school had ordered powdered dyes from India; the students, wearing white clothes, were each given a container of powdered dye and were given the opportunity to cover each other's clothes with these dyes, as a way of celebrating spring. Lastly, it was explained to them how this holiday came into existence as a result of the belief that all people are equal and, by painting each other in all sorts of colors, the differences between the rich and the poor would vanish.

Results of Learning for Life

In modern education, the curriculum rather than the student is often the central focus. This means that teachers must deal with packed schedules and measurable testing objectives that need to be achieved. Within the team at De Parkschool, the awareness grew that worldview education and identity development are important aspects within education, but that these aspects are often difficult to measure and are considered less important as a result. In subjects such as language, arithmetic, and spelling, individual students often receive less attention. Perhaps more so than any other subject, worldview education provides teachers with the opportunity to focus primarily on the student as an individual and to pay close attention to his or her interests and contributions.

The team at De Parkschool states that doing so is valuable, but that it requires an entirely different attitude from the teacher; the reins must be let loose a little because, to an extent, children have a say in what is discussed in class. Through the *Learning for Life* project, De Parkschool has tried to improve in this regard, by philosophizing about different forms of worldview education. The staff has decided to celebrate two Christian, two Islamic, and two "foreign" holidays. Last year, for instance, they celebrated Christmas, Easter, the Sacrifice Feasts, Eid al-Fitr, Holi, and Malala. Holi turned out to be the most educational holiday for the school. The team at De Parkschool is proud of the way Holi was celebrated. They saw a large degree of engagement from their students with both the lessons and the subject in general. The students brought many ideas and stories to the table. Other than that, the team succeeded in employing various teaching formats and reached the conclusion that participating in rituals and contemplating various worldview subjects contribute to an intrinsic engagement from all students.

Staging Dialogical Worldview Education

4.2.3. The Southern Region of the Netherlands

The content of this report about the southern region of the Netherlands is a result of an assignment given to one of our researchers. The assignment was as follows: "Visit three cooperation schools (*samenwerkingsscholen*) and observe two lessons of worldview education. Then engage in a conversation with the students about said lessons. Within our project, we want to find out what students and teachers think of hermeneutical-communicative education."

Cooperation School De Lispeltuut, Oostkapelle

In the small town of Oostkapelle, the Christian primary school and the public primary school have joined forces to collaborate under the banner of De Lispeltuut, a cooperation school participating in the project. Teachers have been involved with the project from the beginning and are using this second year to brainstorm with their colleagues about the way they shape worldview education at their school. In doing so, the hermeneutical-communicative format plays an important role in their exploration of the various possibilities when it comes to integrating world orientation and worldview education.

Getting to Know the Team

Our acquaintance with the team of De Lispeltuut takes place during an afternoon designated for teacher development. Through our talk with Karin and Marijke during this afternoon, it becomes clear to us which steps they have already taken during the first year of the project. Marijke explains how she talked about personal development with her group, which consists of first- and second-year students, during a biology lesson. With the children, she planted seeds in two pots and placed one in a dark and the other in a light environment. By showing the differences in growth between the plants at various stages, Marijke shows the children which kinds of beautiful things can happen if something or someone is given the opportunity to grow. It is a striking analogy for worldview education. Their beautiful stories spark wonder, and wondering is exactly what De Lispeltuut wants its students to do.

Enchanted by Turkey

First, we are allowed to sit in on a class of sixth- and seventh-year students, teacher Marleen's group, for a lesson about Turkey. The lesson was designed based on the lesson plan pertaining to Turkey from the method *Alles-in-1* (all-in-1). This method is structured thematically with the goal of creating coherent education (Alles-in-1, 2016).

On the day we sit in on the lesson, an attack happened in Istanbul. The event provides a lot of food for thought, which is exactly what Marijke hopes to achieve in class. By asking stimulating questions, she wants to give her students the opportunity to form an opinion on what happened. The first part of the lesson is informative, during which Marleen spends a lot of time explaining the cultural differences between Turkey and the Netherlands. By asking the children knowledge-based questions, she attempts to get her group to regard Turkey with an open mind. Afterward, almost all the students we spoke with told us that they enjoyed this part of the lesson. Most children did not know much about Turkey prior to this lesson and are now more informed when it comes to the country and its citizens. The teacher aims to achieve this level of depth in the second part of the lesson, during which the group has a conversation about the freedom of speech.

Being Nice

Ingrid's class, a group of children aged six to eight, is an excited and colorful display, much like Ingrid herself. She starts the lesson on "Being Nice" by having the class sit in a circle and having a plenary conversation with the children. This strikes the students as odd, as they usually work at their seats. During this conversation, Ingrid asks the group several questions, such as what it entails to be nice and whether it is possible to always be nice. Also, Ingrid spends time on general education. She discusses proverbs and sayings with the children which are linked to "being nice": proverbs such as "do not do unto others what you would not have them do unto you." Ingrid and the group discuss what sayings like that mean in the children's daily lives. After class, we reflect. As a teacher, is it easier to link philosophy to a social and emotional theme than to world orientation? Good citizenship appears to be easily linked to the worldview goal of "dealing better with diversity."

Results of Learning for Life

In the group of Ingrid and the group of Marleen, new ways of communication and creative thinking were developed during the lessons. Over the course of this particular lesson, which is primarily aimed at the social and emotional development of the children, worldview depth is achieved using background material that deals with social differences. The children hold a conversation about the theme, and thoughts and opinions are exchanged. From the interviews, it can de deduced that this level of attention for one another is appreciated. An example of this is the fact that one student explains how she enjoyed that, in a circle, you can see and hear each other well. It turns out that the students' open outlook toward one another is literally ensured by the teacher when this approach is used.

In the lesson about Turkey Marleen aimed to achieve a certain depth in the second part of the lesson, using a conversation about freedom of speech. What is striking to us is that this conversation gets off the ground with great difficulty. Even though Marleen asks questions such as "How would you feel if you no longer had access to Facebook?" she is met with little response. No discussion appears to be stimulated. One student, when asked afterward, states that they enjoy having discussions in class. The other children do not mention discussions in any way. This is intriguing. As a teacher, how can you make sure that a world orientation lesson is explicitly made into worldview education? How does a lesson start revolving around finding meaning instead of simply transferring knowledge? Asking only factual questions does not suffice in making a lesson include a discussion on worldview. As a teacher, how can you make sure to ask the right questions at the right times?

Cooperation School De Magdalon, Veere

The second cooperation school we visited was De Magdalon in Veere. At the school, a team was formed, consisting of three teachers and the principal, to further shape worldview education at the school. Teacher Iris and principal Ruud have also been involved in the project since the first year; they take the rest of the team by the hand in their endeavor to teach ways to find meaning and student-centered education.

Getting to Know the Team

Our first acquaintance with a member of the team is with principal Ruud. Prior to our meeting, he sent us a document titled "My First Little Brainwave." The word "little" may make it seem insignificant at first glance, but that turns out to be far from true. It is a very well-thought-out piece on the possible role that (worldview) questions raised by students can play in worldview education. A few weeks later, the series of lessons entitled *Samen Sterk* (stronger together), developed by teacher Iris, is sent to the project group.

The goal of the series is to combine mindfulness, philosophy, and creativity in a cohesive way within ten weeks. Each of the ten lessons is linked to a letter, which combine to form the words "DROOM-GELUK" (dream-happiness). These ten letters represent a fundamental attitude which is prerequisite to being happy: "Doelen" (goals), "Relaties" (relationships), "Openheid en zingeving" (openness and finding meaning), "Opmerken en waarderen" (acknowledgment and appreciation), "Mezelf zijn" (being myself), "Geven" (giving), "Emoties" (emotions), "Lichaam en gezondheid" (body and health), "Uitproberen" (trying out), and "Kracht" (strength).

Leaving Behind

What characterizes worldview education at De Magdalon is the use of the *Trefwoord* teaching method, complemented by teaching formats invented by the teachers themselves. The documents composed by the team mentioned above show that this balance between set outlines and relative freedom forms an important aspect for a possible educational format in the future. This becomes clear during the very first lesson we attend, one that is called "Leaving Behind," which is taught by teacher Carolien to her class of students in their final year of primary school (aged eleven and twelve years). Through various perspectives, Caroline lets her class reflect on the notion of leaving something behind.

She starts the lesson strongly: in a plenary conversation held in a circle. Each student gets to answer the question of what the term "leaving behind" means to them. Not a single child is skipped or glossed over. Afterward, the children note that this is new to them. Usually, only a few children are given the chance to speak, after which the teacher commences the lesson.

By way of closing the conversation, Carolien adds an element from a lesson from *Trefwoord*: the "game of compliments." After all, you can also leave an impression (behind). The children are tasked with leaving a sign expressing a compliment on the back of another student. At the end of the lesson, the children are given the opportunity to go through the compliments, leaving room to self-reflect. During the conversations held with the students afterward, they express that they found the lesson both enjoyable and interesting. Moreover, the children express the fact that they thought it was interesting to look at the notion of "leaving behind" from various perspectives, because the term generally invokes an image of leaving physical objects behind. Two children indicate that the class was calmer than usual; the children listened to one another and participated more actively. After all, paying attention to one another was new in such lessons, according to the children.

On Your Own

After a brief introduction, Inge starts her lesson about "autonomy." First, she and her students brainstorm about the meaning of the word. Inge asks her class what kind of things they can already do on their own, a question that does not require repeating; tying your shoelaces, making a sandwich, or walking to school are only a handful of the responses she was given. In the post-lesson interview, students keep telling about the things they can do on their own. They certainly enjoyed the fact that this question was asked.

During the lesson, Inge connected the word *autonomy* to the biblical narrative of the ascension (Acts 1:9–11). As it turns out, most of the children already knew this narrative. While reading it to the students, she emphasizes the things the disciples need to do on their own now that Jesus is gone. By using this approach, a story the children were already familiar with is given a new dimension. At the end of the story, Inge asked the children: "Would Jesus's friends be able to continue on their own now?" Most students appear to believe they would, after which Inge closes the lesson.

Results of Learning for Life

The interviews conducted with students after each of the lessons are standardized. This means that the interviewers consistently ask the same questions to four-year-olds as they do to twelve-year-olds. During these conversations, it became clear that the youngest students find it difficult to answer these questions. They all profess to have enjoyed the lessons, but they have trouble in explaining why they did. The majority indicates that they believed the biblical narrative was a valuable addition to the lesson, although two children admit to finding it difficult to sit still for such an extended amount of time. What is interesting is that Inge has incorporated the narrative in the *Trefwoord* lesson. In doing so, she connects a traditional narrative to the theme discussed in class, which further emphasizes the worldview dimension of autonomy.

Cooperation School De Stroming, Middelburg

Cooperation school De Stroming is situated in Middelburg. Two of its teachers participated in the first year of the project; in the second year, teacher Henk and principal Lyanne joined them. At De Stroming, students and their parents can choose between the subjects of philosophy and world orientation. Henk teaches the latter. The school is searching for a new way of teaching worldview education, which is in line with the diversity of the students and their parents. The child-centered nature of the hermeneutical-communicative model is appealing to the school.

Getting to Know the Team

We meet Henk during a meeting with the other two participating schools. He passionately tells us about his experiences in worldview education. However, Henk does believe a change is required on a worldview level, now that the school's demographic is changing. How can such a heterogeneous group of children and parents be satisfied? Some of the parents think the curriculum too easily tends to become too Christian, whereas others believe it is not Christian enough.

The Ascension

The first lesson on which we sit in is one taught to students in the last two years of primary school, pertaining to the Ascension of Jesus. The method Henk usually employs, *Trefwoord*, suggests giving a lesson like the one Henk gave last week. This week, he has designed a lesson relating to the biblical narrative himself; we are curious to see the hermeneutical-communicative work formats he came up with. It turns out that the children need to compare biblical narratives.

Afterward, the children indicate that they found the part which contained the biblical narratives the most enjoyable. Of course, this is good to hear, so why are we worried about this part of the lesson? On our way home, we realize that such positive responses probably make changing the curriculum more difficult for a school. What motivates a teacher to change worldview education when the children are content? After all, many teachers are used to years of teaching a form of education which is geared toward the initiation of students into a certain tradition through a model based on knowledge transfer.

Time

A few weeks later, we return at De Stroming to sit in on another lesson taught by Henk. Henk introduces the lesson on "time," inspired by one from *Trefwoord*. The lesson consists of several work formats, all of which are interactive. An interesting part of this lesson was Henk's telling of a biblical narrative relating to time. Henk is a great narrator and the children listen attentively. Afterward, the children are divided into groups and they get to discuss what they believe is the moral of the story. As it turns out, this is not a simple task; it takes a while for the group to get going. However, the ensuing answers are all very interesting to hear: "There is a time for everything", "each day is different," "take your time," or "there is plenty of time, so don't do everything at the same time."

Results of Learning for Life

In De Stroming the students learn to wonder about worldview questions. The children are given the opportunity to muse on the subject together. Henk has managed to turn an abstract subject like "time" into a worldview lesson. The conversations that follow cause the students to wonder. How interesting it is to hear

Staging Dialogical Worldview Education

their ideas about the lesson. During the conversation, the following question was asked: "If you could ask a question about time, what would it be?" We are met with well-thought-out, worldview responses such as: "Why does time exist?" and "Would people understand if I take the time to do something and arrive late for an appointment as a result?" To the team responses such as these prove that a hermeneutical-communicative model for education is important. It challenges children to think about subjects close to their hearts. The subject does not need to relate exclusively to religion; it can also relate to (everyday) life.

4.3. DATA, META-ANALYSIS, AND RESULTS FROM LEARNING FOR LIFE

In the previous section, we presented some examples of specific results of our project in the context of the lived practice of the nine participating schools. In this section, we present the results from a meta-analysis of the data. We have collected data to collate the research and learning processes of the teachers in the PLCs. In addition to other results, like sample lessons, curriculum suggestions and other products, we wanted to see how the hermeneutical-communicative model was appropriated. In the first year of the project, we had all teachers write case studies about the ways in which they had examined their own teaching, and then improved on and evaluated it. They also filled out personal reflection forms for each meeting of the PLC, and also at the end of the year. The researchers also submitted their own observations as material for the research project. The data from the three regions and nine schools (North, Central, and South) were gathered for a cross-case analysis. The PLC facilitators made a summary of all data by region according to a protocol. We then wrote a meta-analysis comprising all data from all over the country. In the second year, we asked teachers for a self-assessment. In terms of procedure, we did the same as in the first year: the PLC facilitators produced a summary according to a protocol. Then the two authors wrote a meta-analysis that comprised all data from all over the country. In the second year, we asked teachers for a self-assessment. In terms of procedure, we did the same as in the first year: the PLC facilitators made a protocolled summary and we wrote a meta-analysis on this basis. In the next two sections, we present the outcomes of these meta-analyses.

In the first year we examined two main questions. First, how did the teachers improve their practice with the aid of the hermeneutical-communicative model (4.3.1)? The second main question was: how do teachers acquire the model while learning in the PLC context (4.3.2)? Both questions are divided into several sub-questions. We analyze the self-assessments of the teachers regarding the second year in section 4.3.3.

4.3.1. Conclusions on Improving Practice Using the Hermeneutical-Communicative Model

How did the teachers improve their practice with the aid of our model? We focused on six sub-questions to operationalize this main question: (1) What are the similarities and differences in educational challenges? (2) Which explanations are presented for these challenges? (3) Which interventions are found? (4) How do teachers motivate these interventions? (5) What are the substantive assessments? (6) What are competence development aspects on which the teachers reflect?

Sub-question 1: Conclusions Regarding the Similarities and Differences in Educational Challenges:

We found several descriptions of challenges in the task of guiding children from the perspective of worldview toward their own perspective on worldview. The challenges are located at the level of the school, but also at the level of teachers.

Staging Dialogical Worldview Education

At the School Level:

1. Despite the different context, public schools, Protestant Christian schools, and cooperation schools all ask how stories, themes, and questions of life from philosophical traditions can be presented in worldview education.
2. Teachers are wondering what place the worldview education or religious education can have at a cooperation school and how this can be put into practice.
3. Also, in public and private contexts, the question is raised of possibilities within the hermeneutical-communicative model to improve the involvement of colleagues, parents, and students regarding the school identity.
4. Public schools formulate the question of how the philosophical dimension, present in all school subjects, can be better expressed by teachers and discovered by students as a contribution to worldview education.
5. Both a Christian and a public school pose the question of how the celebration of a religious feast as an identity marker of the school can connect all students, teachers and parents.
6. Multiple schools raise the question of how curiosity, reflection, posing questions, and the practice of dialogue can contribute to the worldview development of all students and teachers (vision of life, way of life, dealing with philosophical and religious sources).

At the Teacher Level:

1. Some Protestant Christian teachers bring the question to the fore of how Bible stories can become more meaningful to students in relation to their questions of life by working with the hermeneutical-communicative model.
2. Teachers formulate multiple learning questions about the didactical roles from the hermeneutical-communicative

model: role model, guide, coach and imaginator. How can these roles be appropriated personally and contextually?

3. A teacher asks whether creativity is essential for the spiritual development of children and how this could be used fruitfully.

4. Several teachers wonder how to converse philosophically, and which teacher competencies are required for philosophizing about worldview. These questions apply to spontaneous as well to organized moments in the classroom.

These questions or challenges touch upon the consistency between worldview education and school identity. At all school types, a tension is felt between the conscious insertion of religious content in education and the assumed identity of the school. The tension can be formulated as follows: the identity of the school requires a degree of neutrality (public school / cooperation school) or showing one's colors (Protestant Christian) that does not seem to fit in with the use of content from multiple religious traditions. Public schools and cooperation schools wonder to what extent their neutrality is preserved, while Protestant Christian schools may wonder to what extent the Christian character of the school remains assured.

Sub-question 2: Conclusions on the Explanations Provided for the Educational Challenges:

The teachers provide six explanations:

1. According to Protestant Christian teachers, the challenges are, among other things, generated by the diminished religious socialization of children and their religious illiteracy.

2. Some of the schools refer to a lack of detailed vision of worldview education, for instance translated into a learner-centered approach to the subject, as the main cause.

3. Some of the teachers named deficits in teacher competence in respect of teaching worldview education according to the

Staging Dialogical Worldview Education

hermeneutical-communicative model, as well as shortage of preparation time, and a lack of time to consult colleagues.

4. The existing practice generates insufficient involvement by students, parents, and colleagues in curious, creative, and interactive worldview education and in the school's dynamic identity development process.

5. During all kinds of educational renewal projects, a strong desire emerged to start a project that would really lead to in-depth learning in all school subjects and projects at one school.

6. The merging of two schools into a cooperation school creates space when no choice has been made for a teaching method for worldview education. This raises the question of how to teach world orientation from a worldview perspective.

Sub-question 3: Conclusions Regarding Designed Interventions:

1. A colorful palette of interventions is carried out using many methods through which students could respond to worldview content.

2. Much attention has been paid to the practicing of dialogue in the classroom (posing questions, learning to listen, expressing yourself), in which the questions, views, and experiences of the children were central.

3. Lessons have also been tested in which the creative processing of content and the creative responses to content are major changes. These are lessons in which, in particular, the didactical role of the imaginator is used.

4. At the school level, rituals are designed after an intensive dialogue between the school and parents.

Sub-question 4: Conclusions Regarding the Motives for the Designed Interventions:

1. The key word in most of the answers is involvement: teachers want to increase the involvement of students, teachers, and parents all together regarding worldview education.
2. The second motive is the aim of putting the existential questions of children related to their worldview development up front.
3. The third motive is socialization: teachers find it important for children to acquire the faculty to dialogue in view to the diversity in society.
4. Worldview education should also be more meaningful.
5. The interconnectedness of teachers, parents, and children on the theme of worldview should be increased by means of group rituals.

Sub-question 5: Conclusions Regarding the Evaluation of the Interventions:

1. The lecturers are enthusiastic about the ways in which children respond to the new interventions: they discover the many possible thoughts of children, their skills to express themselves creatively, the links between phenomena they now describe, and the originality they show.
2. Teachers are enthusiastic about the increased involvement of students with the theme, which is caused by the hermeneutical-communicative approach.
3. Teachers appreciate the greater commitment of colleagues and parents to the joint brainstorming and organizing of religious celebrations.
4. It was established that learning to formulate existential questions—which are the starting point of the model—is a

Staging Dialogical Worldview Education

difficult task for children, as are the ability and practice of listening to each other's stories.

5. Teachers also must learn competencies regarding moderating a dialogue or philosophizing with children.
6. The hermeneutical-communicative model is an excellent fit in an educational vision that focuses on the development of the child.
7. There are many opportunities for a philosophical conversation at spontaneous moments. Philosophical guidance is part of a pedagogical approach throughout the whole week at school and is not restricted to certain lessons.
8. Hermeneutical-communicative learning is a deeper way of learning, but also more time-consuming in preparation and implementation.
9. Teachers have acquired more knowledge working with the hermeneutical-communicative model than would have been the case working with other models.

Sub-question 6: Conclusions regarding the Competence Development Aspects on which Teachers Reflect:

1. The teachers have discovered that there are several conditions for good worldview education:

    a. Attentivity for moments throughout the day: there are opportunities if you sense them;

    b. The teacher is expected to show willingness to listen, attention, and empathy, and the group must offer security and space for autonomy;

    c. Teaching worldview requires general teaching skills paired with a vision on new aims, new subjects, and space for children, possibly implying a rediscovery of children.

2. There remain some challenges for teachers to meet in the second year of the project:

   a. How do I discover children's questions of life and how can I become sensitive to these existential questions, hidden in the quotidian conversations in the classroom?

   b. How can I appropriate the hermeneutical-communicative model more broadly, for example in stressing other didactical roles, or how can I differentiate better between the various worldview faculties of students?

   c. How can I improve my skills to facilitate dialogues between children, in distinction to a discussion. How can I improve my faculties in choosing the right questions?

   d. How to manage the time-consuming aspect of the hermeneutical-communicative model?

   e. How can we implement the hermeneutical-communicative model at a team level and at a school level?

4.3.2. Conclusions on the Appropriation of the Hermeneutical-Communicative Model within the PLC Context

Our second main question in our meta-analysis in the first year was: How do teachers acquire the model while learning in the PLC context? Again, we focused on several sub-questions to assess this subject: (1) What questions do teachers pose to themselves? (2) What are the key moments in the learning process? (3) What do they receive as a gift from the hermeneutical-communicative model? (4) Which interventions by supervisors were helping?

Staging Dialogical Worldview Education

Sub-question 1: Conclusions on the Questions Formulated by the Practitioners:

1. The teachers pose questions addressing a broad range of aspects from the hermeneutical-communicative model: what is the content, what specific approach is required; the appropriation of roles; what the added value is; how they can connect the hermeneutical-communicative model to their existing approach, e.g., in projects.

2. The teachers also point to the necessity of finding support: how do they get the team, parents, and the school involved in this renewal?

3. The teachers ask questions on the impact of the model on the rest of their education: can other classes benefit from this approach? Are there ways to integrate themes by approaching them from different angles and disciplines?

4. The teachers are wondering how to achieve the time investment required for this project.

Sub-question 2: Conclusions about Key Moments in the Learning Process:

1. Recognition of the learning needs by the teacher based on her or his experience with the current unsatisfying practice and acknowledgment of the desire to leave the existing approach (methodology or method) behind. This is in a way a painful process and requires a mental shift when it comes to orientation point, goals and roles.

2. Awareness and recognition of the teacher roles, the student faculties in worldview learning and the various forms in which worldview can be offered in practice.

3. The operationalization of all the terms and aspects of the hermeneutical-communicative model in the PLC meeting by

giving examples and moderating discussions. There was a lot of communal learning from each other going on.

4. Discovery of the broad scope of the hermeneutical-communicative perspective. It comprises all kinds of sources of meaning, be it from popular culture or from ancient traditions.

5. Awareness of the importance of sensitivity to learning questions from children.

6. Experience of the effects of the hermeneutical-communicative model on teaching and the responses of children in their own practice.

Sub-question 3: Conclusions about the Value of the Hermeneutical-Communicative Model for the Teacher:

1. Teachers find this to be a concrete model that greatly helps in planning, execution, and evaluation of worldview education.

2. Teachers see as a risk that the model easily can be applied too superficially, so critical and thorough application is required. The model is comprehensive and comprises more than some didactical tips and tricks.

3. Teachers state that the hermeneutical-communicative model provides a grip on your own practice by the clear demonstration of concepts and aspects (roles, student faculties, forms, sources, aims).

4. The model helps to put the student back at the heart of the learning process.

5. The teachers appreciate that the model broadens the concept of worldview education by pointing to learning moments outside the classrooms (in the hall, at the playground). They also are inspired by the possibilities of teaching worldview education in other subjects (history, geography, arts, language, citizenship).

6. The hermeneutical-communicative model improves the quality of education, provided that sufficient investment in time and preparation is guaranteed; a second requirement is that teachers must be motivated to improve their own skills.

Sub-question 4: Conclusion on the Interventions of the Supervisors:

The participants designated seven interventions that best supported their learning process:

1. The interventions that explained the aspects of the hermeneutical-communicative model.
2. The interventions asking teachers to reflect upon their existing practice using concepts from the hermeneutical-communicative model (redefining their practice).
3. The interventions that invited to critical reflection from the hermeneutical-communicative model on proposed innovations of their practices.
4. Practicing posing questions.
5. The guidance in walking the steps of the Research Cycle that teachers used to design and report on their case studies.
6. Questions that invited sensitive perception of the practice from the perspective of worldview.
7. Questions and opinions that helped in strategic thinking about team and school development and implementation of the hermeneutical-communicative model at a higher level.

4.3.3. Results from Year 2: Looking Back on the Project

All participants wrote a self-assessment report. We asked them several questions: What did they learn from working on lesson blocks and programs within the hermeneutical-communicative model and related to programs of other disciplines? To what extent did they realize the different structural aspects of the model (dimensions, roles, faculties, aims, existential questions asked by children) in practice? Which questions did they ask themselves? And what are their remaining learning goals? The analysis of the self-assessments of the teachers leads us to ten conclusions:

1. At each school, an awareness and *learning process starts*; how this process is shaped depends on the context of the school, the identity, and the way in which worldview education is organized. The hermeneutical-communicative model lends itself to innovation in all sorts of contexts in all types of private schools (Protestant Christian, Roman Catholic), in cooperation schools, and in public schools. The model can successfully be introduced in all forms of primary education.

2. How *successful* this innovation with the hermeneutical-communicative model can be depends on several factors that we formulate questions wise:

- Is there more support in the team than that of the PLC participants only?

- How is the hermeneutical-communicative model being introduced: as a type of education that is offering space for new forms and perspectives, or as an innovation that threatens existing practices and identities?

- How much room is there to implement the model contextually in a dialogical developmental process?

- To what extent do all teachers become partakers in the process?

- Is there a way in which existing developments, such as personalized learning, philosophizing with children, thinking in multiple intelligences, can be connected or integrated in the hermeneutical-communicative innovation?

- How can we re-assess the particular school identity and the traditions out of which the school has come forth?

Staging Dialogical Worldview Education

- How much room for learning is there at the teacher's level to change vision and attitude and to acquire worldview teaching skills?

3. *Key* for innovation is consistently thinking from the viewpoint of the existential questions and worldview faculties of children. The space for their own quest for meaning and for formulating their own answers differs per teacher and per school. Each school has shifted to the perspective of the child as an anchor point for the education. Existing practices are critically evaluated from this point of view. At some schools, the teaching method is no longer leading, and room has been made to design and implement teachers' own lessons.

4. The *four didactical roles are illuminating* in reflecting on teacher activity; in particular the role of stimulator is tempting, but also challenging: according to the hermeneutical-communicative model, the teacher should shift positions in a dynamic way from supplier (guide), to coach, to role model, to imaginator who invites children to respond. Although the role of coach or supervisor was recognized by every teacher, each role—known or new—challenges the teacher at the point of balance: are the four roles used in an optimal relationship to each other? In reflection, teachers should ask themselves, e.g., how much do I share as a role model and when is it appropriate to do so? Do I explain too much, as a guide, or should I leave more room for discovery? Do I lose myself in all kinds of assignments, without staying focused on the goals?

There should be a certain balance or equilibrium between the roles, taking into account that each teacher has acquired a personal preferred position in the course of his teaching years. The teacher needs to be aware of that preference to be able to choose freely between the four roles.

5. To be able to provide hermeneutical-communicative worldview education, the teacher must have *specific knowledge and skills*, combined with an open and sensitive attitude. Each teacher has to have basic knowledge in the field of worldviews, and an active curiosity about sources and traditions that are needed to ask topical questions to explore. A condition for the acquisition of this

Learning for Life

competence is that reflection on the teacher's own professional concepts and identity.

6. Thinking about the development of a *curriculum* on worldview education has led the teachers of all schools to the conclusion that worldview education is not only confined to a separate field of knowledge, but rather that it is connected to or intertwined with other areas of childhood development. There is a coherence with social emotional development, with philosophy, with rituals, with moral formation, and the broader cultural formation of each student. Worldview education according to the hermeneutical-communicative model lends itself particularly well for *transdisciplinary or interdisciplinary activities*: e.g., art, history, geography, English, philosophy, and citizenship offer clues for the wording of philosophical questions. Specialized or separate classes in religion or worldview are not always necessary.

7. The *structure* of worldview education differs per school. Looking at the learning objectives of hermeneutical-communicative worldview education (see chapter 3), we can say the following:

Objective 1: Personal Clarification of Existence: This objective is shared by all the schools and we can see a change from subject-oriented to child-oriented education. The extent to which this change in perspective stretches varies per school, although the importance of this shift is acknowledged by every school.

Objective 2: Dialogical Handling of Plurality: At some schools, this aim is strongly recognizable as a learning objective in the new lessons and programs, while at other schools this is hardly or only latently the case. This fact is related to the skills of teachers in formulating specific questions to foster dialogue (questions of empathy, changing of perspective, role taking), and to an inviting attitude toward the formulation of existential questions by students. To what extent does the teacher have a natural curiosity about the input of the students, and is the teacher aware of the stratification in diversity in the classes, even if they seem to be "white" or "black"? At the Protestant Christian schools, this learning objective is not pursued as strongly in working forms

Staging Dialogical Worldview Education

and assignments as in the public schools, cooperation schools, or Catholic schools.

Objective 3: Worldview Literacy: Regarding the fostering of worldview and religious literacy, schools provide a varied picture. Some Protestant Christian schools choose the Bible as the main source, with a cautious openness to, for example, the Qur'an. Other Protestant Christian schools offer the children a wide orientation in various religious traditions. Also, we see an embarrassment or hesitation from teachers in public schools about actively introducing worldview sources.

This varied picture is related to the beliefs or questions teachers have on the provision of worldview. They ask themselves: "When children read the Qur'an during class, does that mean that I am transferring Islam?" "When we have a Christmas ritual with Bible readings at our public school, does that mean that we lose our neutrality?" These questions reflect that an active and broad usage of multiple religious and worldview sources depends on choices about identity made at team and school levels. Finally, teachers also point out that they have insufficient knowledge of worldview sources and also insufficient familiarity with the use thereof in learning processes.

8. When it comes to implementation of the *structural aspects* of the hermeneutical-communicative model, we see that the roles of the teacher have been applied in a wide range of variety, but that there is little awareness of the possibility and challenge of differentiation between faculties of students (column 1 from our model, see chapter 3). The faculties to perform a dialogue and to reflect on arguments are activated in various programs and lessons. The other five faculties—"observing," "wondering," "imagining," "telling," "valuing," and "acting"—occur less often and less explicitly. This varies per school and is partly dependent on dimensions of worldview that are presented in the lessons. Every dimension has the possibility to be didactically connected to a variety of faculties, so each lesson about for instance rituals may be different because of the goals set by the teacher. This rich variability has not always been utilized. There are, however, examples of schools,

where teachers more or less by chance, create a new combination. One public school, for instance, combined reflecting, performing a dialogue, and observing, using all three in a lesson where paintings were used as a source of worldview. Another example is a school in which worldview education was built around celebrating feasts. The ritual dimension was used to stimulate the faculties of acting, reflecting, and observing. There is still plenty of room for schools to play even more with new combinations of students' faculties in working with a specific dimension from the Smart model, for instance in a follow-up process.

9. There is also little variation in usage of the *dimensions* (according to the classification of Ninian Smart). Most of the time, rituals, stories, or art forms are chosen in the lesson blocks. The social dimension, the experiential dimension, the philosophical and the ethical dimensions of worldview and religions appear less often in the programs and lesson blocks. Perhaps this is due to the fact that these teachers of worldview education lack experience in applying the Smart classification in their teaching. The social dimension is insufficiently present in the lessons; perhaps this can be linked to our observation that discourses about the worldview development of each student in the PLCs addressed this subject as an individual process. These teachers do not stress a social or relational perspective on religion and worldview. The experiential dimension is less used because there is still insufficient awareness of the experiences of young people concerning worldview in daily life. The philosophical and ethical dimensions are addressed sparsely, perhaps because of insufficient knowledge about students' cognitive development and about students' moral development related to worldview development.

10. The students generally respond *positively* to the new approach to education. Their perception is that a direct appeal is made to their faculties, their experiences, their views, and their actions. They can do something, they know something, their experiences are valued as worthwhile, and they are allowed to share them with each other. They construct their own learning process and outcomes. A wide variety of methods is used, which can be

Staging Dialogical Worldview Education

summed up under the term "activating didactics." In contrast to the "normal" lessons, students indicated that they really learned something.

4.4. THE MODEL: DID IT WORK?

Looking back at two years of action research within this project and at two years of action research preceding this project, we can make some general observations. Although we varied in regional context and in school type, we cannot claim to have arrived at valid general statements which might predict the effects and qualities of the model when appropriated elsewhere. Action research is too contextual and local to be used in that way. Its aim is of a different kind: to improve practices of professionals themselves describing real-life situations in depth, with all the limitations and peculiarities. We can, however, share some observations which may be developed into hypotheses ready to be probed in further research.

Did the model work? Yes, according to the teachers involved: all of them state relevant and major changes in their practices, in the perspective of their contextual learning questions. Yes, according to us as researchers, when it comes to a development in the direction of child-centered education. And with some surprise, we add: it works in all school types in primary education, private, public, and cooperation schools, with diverse identities.

What does it do? It directs the attention in education to the existential questions of children and their own worldview learning processes—instead of directing the main attention to cognitive learning objectives from textbooks, catechesis, and so forth; it brings together the developmental faculties of children, didactical roles of teachers, aims of worldview education, and dimensions of worldview sources in a clear and coherent way. This model is intended as a reference point for educational practices in worldview education, which teachers can return to reflect on and evaluate their lessons and interventions. It works as a matrix for assessing lessons, lesson blocks, programs, and the curriculum as a whole.

Learning for Life

The model has shown to be flexible in serving totally different school contexts. Within the model, typical questions asked at public and private schools can be addressed, and answers are found in experiments. Although the model is normative in its pedagogical starting point (student's life questions) and in the basic concepts of hermeneutics and communication (hermeneutical refers to promoting attention to religious and nonreligious worldview sources, while communicative is about fostering dialog), teachers of all these school types feel that there is room for a particular and contextual appropriation. They all concur on the three aims of the model but differ in the application. This room for school identity conformity in the appropriation is needed and fits the dual school system in the Netherlands. With the aid of this model, Christian and non-Christian schools can prepare their student for a culturally and religiously very diverse society.

We also observe that our work is not finished. First, many schools say they need more time to fully implement the model. At some schools, the shift to hermeneutical-communicative thinking and working needs a lot of individual, team, and school reflection. In a two-year project they claim to come one year short. Second, the hermeneutical-communicative model requires knowledge and didactical skills that exceed the qualifications of a bachelor's degree in education. This means that additional training programs must be developed about religious and worldview sources, didactical roles, and the faculties of children. Third, we need to give more attention to the development of worldview education at public schools. Although we see corresponding learning questions between public and private teachers, for instance how to address religious polarization in society as a theme in the classroom, we also sense that the implementation of the hermeneutical-communicative model requires more reflection and structural adjustments in public schools than in private schools. The latter have a long tradition of offering religious education, and the implementation of the hermeneutical-communicative model means a shift in orientation, not in policy. Public schools did not offer education of this type in the schools, and one can imagine that this innovation

Staging Dialogical Worldview Education

may generate resistance: at the least, it will raise some fundamental questions for teachers, parents, school boards, and policy makers. Fourth, the dynamic interplay between the aspects of the hermeneutical-communicative model could be clarified more. A lot of questions have to be explored further, e.g., can the existential questions of children be classified and connected to preferred dimensions of worldview sources? How do the didactical roles relate to each other, and are there preferred positions to stimulate specific student faculties in the learning process? In short: the hermeneutical-communicative model needs further development, grounded on theory and empirical evidence.

We can say—as far as we can see now—that the model answers the challenge of the secularized and pluralized Dutch society.

Chapter 5
Requirements for Teachers and Teams to Meet the Challenge

IN OUR HERMENEUTICAL-COMMUNICATIVE MODEL, we promote the evolution from a transfer-oriented model of worldview education to a model oriented to students' existential questions. We defined four didactical roles for this task. In this chapter, we focus specifically on the competences that are required for teachers to be able to fulfill the roles to chaperone this dialogical form of worldview education. This theme includes both role-transcending competences and role-specific competences. We point out three cardinal tensions (5.1) and we discuss the competences and roles in 5.2. At the end of this chapter, we pay attention to the special responsibility of the management teams of schools (5.2.2). This responsibility encompasses offering room for experimentation with new forms of worldview education, as well as collaborating with team members toward a shared vision on dialogic worldview education.

Requirements for Teachers and Teams to Meet the Challenge

5.1. THREE FIELDS OF TENSION IN THE TRANSITION FROM TRANSFER-ORIENTED TOWARD STUDENT-ORIENTED WORLDVIEW EDUCATION

In these volatile times in primary education, it seems private and public schools have grown accustomed to old practices and hold on to them because they are familiar. Thus, although student populations changed drastically and are increasingly differentiated socially, culturally, and in their worldviews, these changes have not led teachers to adjust their practices in worldview education. Compared to other parts of the curriculum, teachers in both school types experience a lack of time and space to develop a different method of worldview education. For example, language and history are often taught in a setting of cooperative and investigative learning. These courses are created in a learning environment that is challenging, interactive, creative, and reflective for students. Why would this approach be incompatible with worldview education? What would happen if students would get time and space to research a topic, source, or important question? In the past seventeen years, experimental hubs with new kinds of worldview education have popped up. However, nationally these hubs are limited to a few audacious schools that take on the challenge to design worldview education from the perspective of the student. Furthermore, only a small group of teachers within both school types have shown the guts to explore the rich world of religion and worldview education together with students, working in an open and curious way.

Our reports on the nine schools (chapter 4) gave an impression of the goals of each of the schools within the central focus of hermeneutical-communicative learning. The meta-analysis shows that transforming religious education from a model of transfer focused on the subject matter (tradition-oriented) toward a model in which the student is centralized (student-oriented) is not an effortless process. By this, we mean it is a slow process in which teachers, students, and managers lived through intense situations

Learning for Life

where learning stopped or where interventions missed the mark and did not achieve their desired effect. At the same time, all those involved experienced beautiful and powerful situations, golden moments. Sometimes the eyes of students flickered, and teachers felt empowered in their professional roles. At other times, in the same learning process, there was a sense of resistance and loss of energy in both students and teachers.

The transition from a tradition- and transfer-oriented model toward a student- and meaning-oriented model in worldview education is complex—for students, for teachers, and for the school as a community. We discuss three fields of tension that came to light in *Learning for Life*:

1. The tension between time and space given to each model and the design of worldview education within that model.

2. The tension between the program focused on transferring knowledge and the program focused on the attribution of meaning by students.

3. The tension between the competences and roles of teachers in transferring knowledge from valuable traditions and the competences and roles in stimulating students to learn worldview education in an interactive, creative, and associative manner.

These fields of tension are all related to the normative acts of a teacher as a professional in this transition. In our project, we gained insights in the empowering and interfering moments of a teacher's actions as a normative professional. During her educational practice, each professional constructs a personal interpretive framework, based on which she takes decisions from day to day.[1] In a pilot project, Van den Berg collected examples of good practices.[2] To each of the three tensions, we add an example of a

---

1. Kelchtermans, *De Professionele Ontwikkeling*, 202; Castelijns and Van den Berg, *Een Leraar Blijf Je Altijd*.
2. Van den Berg, *Speelruimte voor Dialoog en Verbeelding*.

Requirements for Teachers and Teams to Meet the Challenge

good practice from this project in which the tension is handled in a creative way.

5.1.1. Tension between Time, Space, and Design

In designing student-oriented worldview education, teachers experience both opportunities and obstacles. They are used to give form to worldview education in a short period of time. An often-heard statement after the ritual of the morning service or moment of contemplation is "now we can get to work." However, transforming worldview education from tradition-oriented toward student-oriented requires time and space for experimentation. Really getting to know students requires taking time and creating space.

Protestant schools' worldview education is often limited to the start and the end of the day. Teachers decide on the amount of time set apart to focus on worldview education, which generally ends up being no longer than thirty minutes. Most of the time, a quarter of an hour is used. This situation provides students with minimal time to respond and ask questions. In practice, we learn that teachers easily drop the subject or moment, because of the amount of pressure it places on other courses such as language and mathematics.[3] Furthermore, a general method for worldview education is often absent.

Example of a Good Practice

Students received a worksheet on which they could fill in what their thoughts were on the Bible narrative about the prophet Amos (from the Old Testament). In this way, a personal connection was constructed with the narrative and ideas were gathered for the "game with the chair" (dramaturgical method). The narrative was played via a CD and children were listening attentively. The narrative from Amos 8 took place in a market and the CD included market sounds. The day before, students got to know the prophet

---

3. Van den Berg, *Speelruimte voor Dialoog en Verbeelding*.

Learning for Life

Amos. Before the teacher started with a new assignment, she invited the children to retell the story they heard two days before. By listening to their stories, the teacher learned that many children felt connected to the story. Emotions of several characters were expressed in their voices. Then, the children discussed the story in small groups of four (interactive method). They could empathize with the prophet Amos and connected his acts to their own reality due to the teacher's question: "Did you ever stand up for anyone?" Some of the children's stories were read out loud. The children listened and reacted to each other. Afterward, the children were assigned to create questions themselves; in the game that followed, these proved to be very surprising questions. During the game, children were seated in a circle. In the middle of the circle there was a chair (dramaturgic method). The teacher sat down on the chair and told the class who she was (a market salesman). Children could ask her questions. After this, a lot of children also wanted to sit on the chair. The children were clearly enjoying the game. In her notes, the teacher stated that this method encouraged the greatest involvement by children. For example, one student had a different perspective on "the wife of the prophet," a perspective the other children did not think of. This changed the perspective of the other students on the story. "This method instigated the enthusiasm of the children, but also my own enthusiasm," states the teacher. "The narrative opens up in a lively and creative interaction."[4]

Conclusion

The time and space necessary for student-oriented and context-specific worldview education are not self-evident and need to be conquered on existing practices. Internalized routines in worldview education are not easily breached or changed. In the context of projects where official hours were reserved for teachers to develop new methods, this time and space proved to be used in optimal

---

4. Van den Berg, *Speelruimte voor Dialoog en Verbeelding*, 452–54.

Requirements for Teachers and Teams to Meet the Challenge

ways.[5] Afterward, when things go "back to normal," it is essential to continue the development of the student-oriented approach. In the light of current pressures on primary schools, the question rises whether space, time, and new methods will be secured in worldview education currently. Primary schools are under constant pressure to invest in language, mathematics, examination, and so on. Within this context, limited space is available for creative courses and worldview education. Furthermore, worldview education is often viewed as an unequal subject when compared to other alternatives. These trends combined lead to a situation in which there is no room for the vision that worldview education is a necessary and essential part of the personal identity development, social development, and cultural development of each student.

5.1.2. Tension in Space for Materials and for Students

In the transition from the old to the new approach, teachers develop an understanding of students' own voices. Students develop their own views on life by exploring a valuable source or researching an important question together with others. Most teachers have the tendency, due to their education and their passion, to be the sender of information in class. However, especially in a course such as worldview education, it is important to invite students to contemplate for themselves and to express in words how they feel about a certain character in a narrative. This transition from transferring knowledge to students toward challenging students to explore a valuable narrative or other source is a complex process—complex in the sense that it demands time and practice from teachers. These are necessary to develop an eye and an ear for the voice of each student, for his or her needs and questions in the field of worldview education.

---

5. Parlevliet et al., *Het Kind en de Grote Verhalen*; Van den Berg and Mulder, *Leren van Betekenis*.

Learning for Life

Example of a Good Practice

Teacher Janine narrates: "Esther was living with Mordechai first, and now is living in the palace. Mordechai misses her a lot and walks to the gate every day. He asks how things are going with Esther. He hears two of the king's stable boys talking to each other quietly; they are whispering. The next day the same thing happens. What does Mordechai hear? The two stable boys are mad at the king. Does he hear it correctly?! They want to kill the king." Janine then asks the students: "What would you do?"

    Joanne: "Tell the king."
    Mawjoed: "Get help."
    Elize: "Tell the king and fire them."
    Joram: "Tell the king and give them the death penalty."
    Janine: "Isn't that penalty too harsh?"
    Joanne: "I would go to them and arrest them."
    Marjan: "I would tell the maid, so she can tell the king."
    Michiel: "The palace has a front side and a back door. Go in at the back door and tell the king. And call the police."

Together, the students explore the possible actions that Mordechai's character can take. Seven possibilities are mentioned. In doing so, their perspective on the story is expanded and the students discover sense and meaning in a playful way. Independent thought processes are accelerated by two of Janine's actions: presenting the narrative in an interactive way and asking the right question at the right time. Students are given all the space they need to formulate answers that exist in a parallel to each other. This fragment shows that Janine has acquainted herself with the narrative and that she translates her own connection with the dynamics in the story into her pedagogic method. Furthermore, she explores one of the student's reactions further to deepen the understanding of his reaction.

    Students develop their worldview in the interactions between themselves and others, between cultural forms and their responses to them, and between their own observations and imaginations

Requirements for Teachers and Teams to Meet the Challenge

they encounter in cultural and traditional worldview narratives.[6] A precondition for deep learning by students is the development of mental, creative, and social skills and competences, for example, being able to empathize with someone or something, or to have a dialogue with a (fictive) person.[7] In his studies, Kieran Egan, pedagogue and philosopher, shows that activating these mental capabilities (wondering, imagining, and thinking) and higher mental, creative, and social competences such as dialoguing, symbolizing, philosophizing, and playing play a crucial role in students' personal and worldview development.[8]

Conclusion

New practices sometimes emerge when teachers present a narrative in a different way. When teachers have knowledge of the mental and social capabilities on which they are relying in their interaction with students, and know when to ask the right question, this leads to powerful and beautiful moments of learning for both students and teachers. Knowledge of worldview development in students is an important precondition to be able to do so. Moreover, to prevent teachers from falling back into their old and safe routines, this method requires bravery, audacity, and the ability to handle uncertainty about the direction a class takes.[9]

5.1.3. Tension in Teacher Roles and Capabilities

In student-oriented education, teachers must be able to instigate wonder and curiosity in their students. This means different roles and capabilities are asked of them. This transition is at the heart of the third field of tension.

---

6. Van den Berg et al., *Geloof Je het Zelf?!*
7. Alma, *Grensverleggende Exploratie*.
8. Egan, *Educated Mind; Imaginative Approach; Future of Education*.
9. Parlevliet et al., *Het Kind en de Grote Verhalen*.

Learning for Life

Primary school teachers are educated to be able to provide education fit for the educational needs of their students. In the field of worldview education, up until now teachers have not been equipped to professionally design student-oriented worldview education. A logical fallacy is then to fall back on old practices and routines, following a set method or practicing their own beliefs. Transitioning toward student-oriented education requires teachers to be able to respond to children's questions in a professional pedagogical and didactic manner. Furthermore, it places demands on teachers' capacity for wonder, curiosity, and creativity. In a new learning environment teachers must get acquainted and familiarize themselves with new forms of worldview education, such as philosophizing with children, symbolizing with children, or having conversations with children. Getting used to another approach is a time-consuming and practice-intensive effort and, moreover, requires teachers to let go of old routines and ways of thinking.

Example of a Good Practice

One of the teachers has made an effort to think of a creative way which enables her to encourage very young children to empathize with characters in a narrative, at their own level of development. She took the time and had the courage to explore this no-man's-land for new possibilities and opportunities. In her quest for a new method, she relied on literature which provided her with new insights into ways children aged four to six can establish relations with biblical narratives. In her implementation, she paid extensive attention to the reactions of students and what these reactions required of her dialogical capacities. In doing so, she acknowledged her own enthusiasm in designing new and creative methods for worldview education. This process requires the willingness and mental elasticity to change and break into current processes and create space for a new approach. This transition is not a process that happens overnight, nor inside the teacher's head, nor in her practices. Once developed by professionals such as teachers,

Requirements for Teachers and Teams to Meet the Challenge

practices in thinking, speaking, and acting are not easily interrupted nor transformed.

Conclusion

Narratives become more meaningful for teachers when they create space for themselves to gain a new perspective, by asking different questions or reading the stories with a different mind-set. In doing so, teachers also create an openness and newfound curiosity to react to students' questions or interpretations. Guiding students effectively in their quest for meaning and their path through the no-man's-land of worldview development can only be successful when teachers are prepared to engage with their students. Transitioning from a teacher focused on the transfer of knowledge or the practice of everyday rituals toward a teacher who explores stories in an active, creative, and dialogical way is a hard, yet also beautiful path.

5.1.4. Insights in the Complexity of These Three Tensions

We identified three fields of tension related to the transition from tradition-oriented toward student-oriented worldview education. All three tensions are focused on changes in teachers' professional practices. This section discusses experiences from our projects that are related to these fields of tension.

In relation to the first field of tension, on time and space for the design of worldview education, we can establish that teachers took full advantage of the space for experimentation within all our projects. During the projects, they were able to design powerful methods for student-oriented worldview education. Within this space granted to them, teachers were able to break free of the constraints of existing practices and methods and fully commit to the experiment. The examples of Marina, Janine, and Mirjam described above show this in a unique way. In these experiments, these teachers witnessed beautiful moments, involving students making sense of narratives, as well as their own wise, brave, and creative acts. Some of the teachers in the projects discovered greater space in their field of play when connecting their practices to language and worldview education.[10] One factor that was experienced as stimulating by teachers was the available time and attention for peer-to-peer reflection on their experiments. Due to this, they were more able to gain perspective on certain pedagogic situations in which students did not react as expected, could not concentrate, or were unable to relate to the narrative. Designing student-oriented education is solely possible when teachers have the possibility to break away from day-to-day activities and to cooperate in building worldview education focused on students in their exploration of the world of different cultures and religions. This requires schools to consciously create policy which allows time and space for such experimentation. In turn, it requires teachers to have the guts and sensitivity to make use of this space.

In relation to the second field of tension, room for materials and/or students, it became evident that teachers became more sensitive toward the individual voices of students. This sensitivity developed because they encouraged students to play with the symbolic language of religious narratives. This growing awareness in teachers was strengthened by a deepened insight in and knowledge of children's worldview education. The more specific their questions and assignments to students became, the more powerful the voices of students resonated and the more their eyes started glowing.

Finally, in relation to the third field of tension concerning the teachers' roles and capabilities, it became clear that teachers have discovered and acquainted themselves with new methods. In their role as a professional teacher, they experienced that each creative method demands specific capabilities and the activation of specific capacities. Implementing this transition requires a basic attitude that is characterized by an open, flexible, and engaged attention for the interaction between students and a question, theme, or source. The required attitude encourages them to act in an inventive and

---

10. For examples see Parlevliet et al., *Het Kind en de Grote Verhalen*.

Requirements for Teachers and Teams to Meet the Challenge

assertive way, motivating hesitant students to participate as well. Teachers who can act wisely, bravely and inventively in such situations will dare to take on the challenge and to go on an exploratory journey together with students, learning to interact with students more easily and playfully.

5.2. ROLES AND COMPETENCIES OF TEACHERS

As we described in chapter 3, to kick-start worldview education according to the hermeneutical-communicative approach, every teacher must be able to fulfill the four identified didactic roles at a satisfactory level. In the description of these roles, we were inspired by ideas from Didier Pollefeyt. We have adapted his rather short descriptions to the Dutch situation, translated them into non-confessional terms, and expanded them by adding a fourth role to which we attribute great significance: the imaginator, or stimulator of imagination. In our publications dating from 2016, we use terms for the four roles comprehensible for teachers in both public and special education:

Guide: the teacher guides students through the rich world of cultural worldview and cultural-religious narratives, rituals, values, questions, ideas, and practices. The cultural guide has learned to find their way in this rich world and corrects students' misinterpretations or mistakes based on actual scientific and personal knowledge and insights.

Coach: the teacher supports students in learning how to express and research existential questions and in researching life themes using valuable sources. The teacher supports students in learning how to have valuable dialogues about life themes and in working with a diversity of sources and their interpretations. As a discussion leader, she practices symbolizing, philosophizing, and discussing with the students.

Role model: the teacher is a role model for students in the way she incorporates her personal values, ideals, and motivations into students' quests toward their own worldview, way of life, and attitude. The teacher discloses her beliefs or worldview without aiming to convince students; she shows what she thinks is important and represents how worldview plays a role in her life. She shows what touches her and what speaks to her.

Imaginator: the teacher stimulates the imagination of students. The teacher encourages them to express stories and other types of answers to their encounters with the symbolic language of narratives, rituals and practices from worldview traditions. He encourages activating their own imagination in creative methods and allows students the possibility for self-expression and self-discovery.

These four didactical roles are often connected within a lesson or other learning moment. Different situations ask for different roles, and some will be more useful than others. This depends greatly on the topic under discussion. Does the topic require a lot of background information and knowledge (cultural guide) or is it suitable for a dialogue between students (coach)? Does the topic affect the teacher and is there a possibility to present yourself as a role model in relation to a certain topic? We advise creating an optimal balance between all four roles, to achieve the goals strived for in student-oriented worldview education and to maximize learning possibilities for the student. In practice, teachers will take the imaginator role relatively often, so students are given the space and time to react to the offered content.

5.2.1. General Competence and Specific Competencies of Teachers

Each didactical role requires specific capabilities. Certain competences are role-transcending and belong to the core of each teacher's *professional craftsmanship*. The four roles described assume openness and curiosity for what is going in the world close by and far away, social and communal involvement, and a deep empathy for students, colleagues, and the world outside of school. Apart from this basic attitudinal competence, three role-transcending, general competencies are valuable:

Requirements for Teachers and Teams to Meet the Challenge

The first is the capability to *observe, watch,* and *listen*. In their training and education, teachers practice this competence, but it is a competence which can only blossom and be refined in the everyday practice of teaching. During your career as a teacher, you become a better listener to your students' stories. Furthermore, you learn to grant students the space to stay open for valuable life lessons and life orientation, amid all other impressions and learning. To be able to do so, you need to develop an open conscience; in that context, you preserve openness in watching and listening, despite all the pressures of daily work.

A second role-transcending competency is the use of *freedom* and *boldness* in your actions and communication, freedom to deviate from trodden pathways or routines in exploring existential questions from religious sources with your students. A decisive factor in this context is whether the students' learning process is stimulated in their exploration of a question or source.

A third role-transcending competency, which is of major importance, is the competency to operate in an *open-minded and inventive way*. In concrete teaching situations, this competency allows the teacher to retain the uniqueness of a certain moment, conversation or image.

For each of the four roles, we can also identify role-specific competencies. They are present in obvious ways within the examples described in this chapter and in chapter 4.

As a *guide*, the competency to teach based on wisdom is crucial. Wisdom derives partly from life experience, and partly from knowledge, ability and experiences gained as a professional teacher. This type of wisdom is also known as *tacit knowledge*, born in the ongoing dialogue between teachers with multiple, diverse cultural-worldview traditions. This is the mature conscience of a teacher who stays or becomes open to and curious about the richness of traditions, and who keeps his knowledge and experience up to date to develop his own dynamic professional identity. Furthermore, the teacher should keep obtaining new knowledge and insights from the richness of diverse traditions, present these traditions without prejudice, and let students experience them by themselves.[11] Also important for this role is the competency to be a guardian of truth in worldview narratives and to take responsibility for the truthful voice of the narrative within the process of appropriation. Narratives can be read or interpreted in different ways but are not fit for every line of thinking. Therefore, it is the responsibility of the cultural guide to add context or perspective from the background of a story when students are exploring a narrative.

The role of *coach* requires the specific competence to ask *context-specific* questions to students, questions that invite them to express themselves in words or images, or that enable them to appreciate and understand the expressions of another student. The coach also knows all about dialogue and instructs students accordingly. Another specific competency related to this role is the capability to give students challenging assignments that ask them to share meanings they attribute to religious dimensions that they are researching together. These cannot be standard assignments; instead, they must be specific assignments suited to the specific needs of students and to the richness of knowledge and insights hidden within traditional and modern religious phenomena.

In a teacher's role as a *role model*, the most significant competency is to transfer his own vision or opinion about a religious topic in such a way that students feel free to join in or assign a different meaning to the topic. This requires a strong knowledge of the teacher's own values and ideals that guide his actions and that allow him to act honestly and to the best of his knowledge in concrete learning situations with students. An inspiring way of telling and presenting experiences, by which students can perceive their teacher's passion, offers space and room for different types of students to search for answers using their own activated imagination. The capability to narrate in an enthralling way and to engage students in your narratives is of crucial importance for students, since you broaden and deepen their reality as well as their imagination. This competency also comprises the willingness and

11. OSCE/ODIHR, *Toledo Guiding Principles*, 6-10.

Requirements for Teachers and Teams to Meet the Challenge

ability to be vulnerable and the insight to pick the right moments for witnessing.

The ability to envision, enact, and tell narratives is equally crucial for the *imaginator* role. The more practiced a teacher is in actively symbolizing with a religious narrative, in playing with images and metaphors, the more he will tickle the imagination of students under his care. Imaginative symbolizing with students requires teachers to question their own opinions, motivations, and ideals, and to invite students to respond in a playful way to what is offered, experienced, and discussed in class. The imaginator has knowledge of a multitude of didactical working formats, didactical assignments, and examples that can be used to differentiate between students' faculties to be stimulated. The ability to use creative methods is part and parcel of the teachers' competencies.

5.2.2. Competencies of School Executives

The lived identity of a school community is carried and acted out not only by teachers, but also by people who manage a school as a living network.[12] When a school builds a pedagogical climate in which management and teaching team emphasize the importance of the opportunity for all students, in all their diversity, to develop their own view on humans, world, and life in general, because of and within the learning process, this immediately reflects on the teaching process of the teachers and the learning process of the students. All those involved within a living school community will then experience that the challenge of each school—to prepare students to participate in the society of tomorrow—plays an important role in education and learning processes. Students will then experience the reality of a school that is involved as a community, with their children and parents, close by and from afar.

To achieve the above, people in leadership roles need to develop a strong *sensitivity* to several questions: Which initiatives encourage students to be involved in the experiences and realities

12. Stern, *Spirit of the School*.

of other students? What challenges them to empathize with the lives of students and parents from other countries and cultures? How do you strengthen students' realization that the heart of good education is caring for yourself, for each other and for the world?

School leaders can provide their team members with a larger or smaller professional space to experiment with their students in their search for new methods of authentic and specifically student-oriented and dialogical worldview education. Schools in which managers joined in on the quest for quality worldview education were better able to embed a designed experiment in the organization, as opposed to schools in which the leadership kept their distance. Examples from our projects show this in a powerful way. Furthermore, executives can, together with their teachers, search for ways to develop a school's own vision on student-oriented dialogical worldview education, defined within the specific cultural-worldview context of a school, and for all those involved to acquaint themselves with this vision. This follows from the concept that those providing the education are the carriers and translators of the lived identity of a school.[13]

In Conclusion

Transitioning from tradition-oriented toward student-oriented worldview education is a long-term process, characterized by ups and downs and deserving space and time within each primary school. In this space, teachers can, while learning from both their powerful moments as well as their moments of resistance, develop into wise, bold, and inventive teachers. This requires the willingness of people in leadership positions to break with existing practices and create space for the new student-oriented method of worldview education. It demands resilience for teachers to design this transitory process step by step, create this new form of education, and support students in their exploration of the rich world of worldview, culture, and religion. Teacher Training Centers for

---

13. Van der Harst et al., *Verhalen Verbinden*.

Requirements for Teachers and Teams to Meet the Challenge

primary school teachers should create more space within their program, allowing student teachers to design lessons in which the reality of students and their curiosity about the world of religion and worldview are at the center. Teachers-in-training then deepen and explore the rich world of culture, worldview, and religion, and gain more knowledge and insights about it. At the same time, they learn together with more experienced colleagues to design specific and authentic worldview education.

Reflection

The Road Ahead

WE STARTED OUR JOURNEY with a challenge: how can teachers in religious education deal with the challenge of secularization and religious diversity in Dutch society? The Netherlands are among the most secularized societies in Europe; the country tops the Religious Diversity Index published by the Pew Research Center.[1] In the spirit of recommendations made by the European Union, we developed a model for hermeneutical-communicative religious education that respects the rights of children to construct their own religious identity and that tries to avoid harmful misunderstandings, instead fostering insight and respect between different worldview positions. Indeed, we aim for our model to promote tolerance and respect, not only by directing attention to religious literacy—which is an important guidance from and instrument for the European Committee—but also to attitudinal aspects and skills. How do we look back on our project and our results from the perspective of the development of Europe into a tolerant and peaceful community?

---

1. Pew, "Religious Diversity Index Scores by Country," April 4, 2014 (accessed April 26, 2016), http://www.pewforum.org/2014/04/04/religious-diversity-index-scores-by-country/.

Reflection

A PROMISING MODEL

Working with public and private schools within one practice development group convinced us that our model is a promising model for every type and denomination. We observed that Christian and non-Christian schools faced similar questions raised by the secularizing and diversifying society. It was inspiring for us to see the teachers debate respectfully about issues like the value of religious sources and the adaption of religious feasts, helping each other to clarify their questions. Most of all, the common will to switch from focusing on content to the existential questions of students as a starting point for educational programs convinced us that this model could really work. The appropriation of the model in Professional Learning Communities is a workplace in which respect and dialogue are practiced. Teachers themselves experience in their learning processes what they want to achieve with their students at school.

The model is also promising because it takes the teachers' own worldview positions into account. Nonreligious teachers can work side by side with pious Christians or Muslims. Religious convictions are not a requirement. What is required—following the insights from the European documents (chapter 1)—is an understanding of the nature and the importance of religion and worldview for individuals and communities. Teachers need to be convinced that religious and nonreligious sources, convictions, practices, and artefacts are valuable, that they are connected to personal and communal identities, and that they deserve understanding and respect.

The model is promising because it is open to all kinds of attribution of meaning. Worldview can be religious or nonreligious; existential questions can be interpreted from traditional and institutional perspectives, but also from modern cultural perspectives. Popular culture can be a very important source for people, and the model allows for mining from various sources. Bible readings can be followed the next day by watching a short animated film. In this openness, children experience a welcoming attitude to that

Learning for Life

which is different, that which is strange, that which they do not know. Differing sources of wisdom can be of equal importance and are acknowledged within the classroom. The classroom is a microsociety, preparing students for society at large. We truly believe that development into a peaceful and respectful society can only exist in the bracketing of absolutistic propositions. No religion possesses the truth, yet all are searching for it. With our perspective of happy particularism (chapter 3) we contemplate the colorful ways people find to answer existential questions. The otherness of the other is welcomed as a mirror to our own position. We must acknowledge that the answers and practices between religions and communities sometimes differ so much that they are incompatible and incomparable.[2] We cannot bring them back to one basic form or basic experience. This makes it hard to understand each other. Nevertheless, the only way to peaceful citizenship is the openness to other voices, and the hospitality to that which is strange to our own self. This hospitality is practiced in the classrooms. So, the model is promising because it heads toward depolarization and understanding. In this model, education is not for personal profit, but for teaching students to be democratic citizens.[3] What children need to be able to live in European society is more knowledge of and insight into worldviews and religions and the existential meaning and salience thereof for the people around them.

The model is promising because it addresses the child as a whole being, a person who has more than cognitive faculties. Education is about learning to be human, not only about filling children's minds with information. It also includes touching hearts and setting bodies into motion, and connecting bodies to one another in play, discussion, and action. The model opens the door to paying attention to all kinds of intelligence.

The model is promising because it aims at critical thinking: at discussing, examining, and evaluating what is offered as worldview sources. Teachers have the knowledge to teach children to discern what is fact and what are frames, what is genuine and

2. Moyaert, *Fragile Identities*.
3. Nussbaum, *Not for Profit*.

Reflection

what is falsehood when it comes to portraying religion. Students learn to ask relevant questions, and to weigh the answers within themselves. The model is promising because of the invitation to students to respond to situations, themes, questions, experiences, and stories in their own authentic way. Hermeneutical-communicative learning confidently embraces the concept that children can think, offer answers, and use intuition and reflection in order to grow spiritually. The model does not prescribe answers from any tradition, but instead invites creative response. It aims at self-trust, self-esteem, and self-worth. The model is promising because it supports the use of all kinds of activating didactics. Lessons can be fun, and different learning styles can be addressed and supported. Individual and cooperative assignments lead to learning outcomes that are sometimes individual and at other times social in nature.

Finally, the model is promising because it embeds the opportunity for cooperative innovation. We are grateful to have been able to watch a flow of positive energy emerge in school teams that started renewing their lessons and programs from the perspective of children. A source of creativity can be uncovered when teachers let go of existing methods and reach for new horizons together.

A VULNERABLE MODEL

Looking back, we also have to acknowledge that these promises are at risk to a certain extent. The model itself is vulnerable, just as teaching is vulnerable and teachers are vulnerable.[4]

On the micro-level of the teacher, the model is vulnerable to the teachers' personal abilities to appropriate the model. The three aims of the model must be embraced wholeheartedly. The model is not primarily about didactics. It is a fundamental change of perspective on religious education at all kinds of levels (chapter 3). Some teachers have to make room within themselves to be able to pass thresholds while they reconsider the aims of worldview education. It is not the teachers' beliefs or teaching that are most

---

4. Kelchtermans, *Teachers' Emotions*.

important, but the students' search for meaning, in dialogue with each other. Outcomes are not always predictable. Learning happens in processes over which the teacher does not have full control.

The second risk at this micro-level is insufficient competency. The teacher cannot be expected to know all about the wealth of sources of meaning. The same holds true of the skill of asking the right question in order to put the students in control of their own learning processes. Hermeneutical-communicative teaching requires more than general basic training for primary education. The model is also vulnerable at the level of teams. We learned that instructive conversations and multiple intensive discussions are necessary to reach a common understanding and consensus on the use of the model. By nature, the model needs a contextual implementation. Lessons and programs, courses and events, and rituals should be constructed within the school and team identity. The shift to student orientation cannot be made by one or two teachers: it takes mutual effort and support from the management and school board. For many private schools, religious education is a hallmark of the school identity. Major changes are met with resistance and all kinds of questions. Introduction of the hermeneutical-communicative model has to be done with care.

Third, the model is vulnerable because of its openness and flexibility. Within the boundaries of the three aims, everything is possible. There are no restrictions or prescriptions about filling in the didactical roles or the worldview dimensions. Although we defend a balance between the four roles, and between the dimensions chosen, there are no clear-cut packages that show how to adjust the model to the school context. Schools, teams, and teachers have to find their own way. There is a risk of imbalance, of stressing one's own role or dimension over another. Personal preferences of teachers and teams can have decisive influences that can create one-sidedness. That unilateral perspective must be avoided in order to do justice to the richness of and diversity in religion and worldview and in the learning styles and faculties of students. Teams need critical peers or experts to discover blind spots in their approach and to defend the full spectrum of possible colors.

Reflection

THE ROAD AHEAD

We want to continue pursuing our research. Society needs people with a strong identity that pairs a sense of self-worth and self-consciousness to openness and respect for others. Schools are entitled to support if they would like to work with our model. Does the vulnerability disqualify the model? We think not. Some of the weaknesses are in fact strengths when handled with care. This holds true for the implementation of the model in general. It is a time-consuming process (and therefore costly in a sense) and a school has to choose this road consciously and with determination. If that happens, the promises of the model can come true and the school, teachers, and students will all be enriched by it. With a well-designed implementation plan, a lot of the vulnerabilities can be turned into strengths.

Our research still needs to deepen the model theoretically. In addition, more reflection has to be done on the level of details. The four roles have to be described more extensively and in their co-occurrences. Didactical strategies, developed by teachers working within the model, must be monitored and shared. The students' worldview faculties also have to be described for older children in other grades. And the coherence between the aspects of the model (aims, roles, dimensions, faculties) needs further study and reflection.

Different ways of contextualizing the model have to be described to discover patterns and to be able to advise new schools that want to join us on our journey. We expect to find preferred ways of implementation between denominations; that can be helpful.

Once we have acquired more experience with the model, we can describe the required competencies for teachers in more detail and differentiate between the contexts of private and public schools. With this set of competencies (knowledge, skills, and attitudes), we want to create educational programs to prepare primary school teachers better for this beautiful, challenging, important, and inspiring task: worldview education.

Learning for Life

In conclusion, we need to know more about the existential themes that influence students' behavior. We are convinced that extreme, discriminating, or hostile assertions that are expressed in class are often linked to personal fears or despair and should be addressed from an existential level. That approach will be more fruitful than addressing the assertions at a behavioral or moral level. This knowledge, which is needed in our times, will provide more insights into the souls of children growing up in secular, diverse societies. Knowledge about life questions will contribute to the threefold hermeneutical juggling and will support the worldview educator in creating a powerful learning environment in which children can learn for life.

Appendix A
Toledo Learning Outcomes

THE TOLEDO GUIDELINE DESCRIBES the following learning outcomes for Worldview Education as follows:

- Attitudes of tolerance and respect for the right of individuals to adhere to a particular religion or belief system. This includes the right not to believe in any religious or belief system;
- An ability to connect issues relating to religions and beliefs to wider human rights issues (such as freedom of religion and freedom of expression) and the promotion of peace (i.e., the capacity of religions and beliefs for solving and preventing conflicts);
- A core knowledge about different religions and belief systems and knowledge of the variation that exists within all religions and beliefs, with reference both to the local/national context as well as to larger geographical areas;
- An understanding that there are various legitimate ways to view history and historical developments (multi-perspectivity);
- Knowledge of the contexts associated with major historical events relating to different religions and belief systems; here, again, the specific attention to local/national circumstances

Appendix A

should be combined with a broader geographical and cultural perspective;

- An understanding of the importance of religious or philosophical beliefs in a person's life;
- Awareness of similarities and differences between different religions and beliefs;
- The ability, based on sound knowledge, to recognize and to question existing negative stereotypes about religious communities and their members;
- An historical and psychological understanding of how a lack of respect for religious differences has led to extreme violence in the past and, related to this, the importance of people taking an active role in protecting the rights of others (civic responsibility);
- The ability to counteract, in a respectful and sensitive way, a climate of intolerance and discrimination, when it occurs.[1]

---

1. OSCE/ODIHR, *Toledo Guiding Principles*, 48–49.

Appendix B
Toledo Key Principles for Teaching Worldview Education

IN SUM THE KEY principles for teaching worldview education are:

- Teaching about religions and beliefs must be provided in ways that are fair, accurate, and based on sound scholarship. Students should learn about religions and beliefs in an environment respectful of human rights, fundamental freedoms, and civic values.[1]

- Those who teach about religions and beliefs should have a commitment to religious freedom that contributes to a school environment and practices that foster protection of the rights of others in a spirit of mutual respect and understanding among members of the school community.

- Teaching about religions and beliefs is a major responsibility of schools, but the manner in which this teaching takes place should not undermine or ignore the role of families and religious or belief organizations in transmitting values to successive generations.

- Efforts should be made to establish advisory bodies at different levels that take an inclusive approach to involving

---

1. I OSCE/ODIHR, *Toledo Guiding Principles*, 16–17.

Appendix B

different stakeholders in the preparation and implementation of curricula and in the training of teachers.

- In case a compulsory program involving teaching about religions and beliefs is not sufficiently objective, efforts should be made to revise it to make it more balanced and impartial, but in case this is not possible, or cannot be accomplished immediately, recognizing opt-out rights may be a satisfactory solution for parents and students, provided that the opt-out arrangements are structured in a sensitive and nondiscriminatory way.

- Those who teach about religions and beliefs should be adequately educated to do so. Such teachers need to have the knowledge, attitude and skills to teach about religions and beliefs in a fair and balanced way. Teachers need not only subject-matter competence but pedagogical skills so that they can interact with students and help students interact with each other in sensitive and respectful ways.

- Preparation of curricula, textbooks, and educational materials for teaching about religions and beliefs should take into account religious and nonreligious views in a way that is inclusive, fair, and respectful. Care should be taken to avoid inaccurate or prejudicial material, particularly when this reinforces negative stereotypes.

- Curricula should be developed in accordance with recognized professional standards in order to ensure a balanced approach to study about religions and beliefs. Development and implementation of curricula should also include open and fair procedures that give all interested parties appropriate opportunities to offer comments and advice.

- Quality curricula in the area of teaching about religions and beliefs can only contribute effectively to the educational aims of the Toledo Guiding Principles if teachers are professionally trained to use the curricula and receive ongoing training to further develop their knowledge and competences regarding this subject matter. Any basic teacher preparation should be

Toledo *Key Principles for Teaching Worldview Education*

framed and developed according to democratic and human rights principles and include insight into cultural and religious diversity in society.

- Curricula focusing on teaching about religions and beliefs should give attention to key historical and contemporary developments pertaining to religion and belief, and reflect global and local issues. They should be sensitive to different local manifestations of religious and secular plurality found in schools and the communities they serve. Such sensitivities will help address the concerns of students, parents, and other stakeholders in education.

Appendix C
List of Participants

PROJECT MANAGER

Drs. M. Stroetinga

PARTICIPATING SCHOOLS

Protestant-Christian School De Zevensprong, Dronten
Protestant-Christian School De Es, Hellendoorn
Public School De Carrousel, Dalfsen
Catholic School De Achtbaan, Utrecht
Protestant-Christian School De Parkschool, Utrecht
Public School De Horn, Wijk bij Duurstede
Cooperation School De Lispeltuut, Oostkappelle
Cooperation School De Magdalon, Veere
Cooperation School De Stroming, Middelburg

PARTICIPATING UNIVERSITIES

Windesheim University of Applied Sciences, Zwolle
Marnix Academie University of Applied Sciences, Utrecht
HZ University of Applied Sciences, Vlissingen

Appendix C

PARTICIPATING RESEARCHERS

All participating teachers of the nine schools and their interns

Dr. B. van den Berg
A. den Herder, MA
Drs. R. Hessel, MA
Dr. J.G. Lambregtse
Dr. A. Mulder
Dr. L.-J. Parlevliet
Drs. I. van Ruler-Oosterkamp
J. Slingerland-Van de Hoef, MA

Bibliography

Alii, E. T. *Godsdienstpedagogiek. Dimensies en Spanningsvelden.* Zoetermeer, Netherlands: Meinema, 2009.
Alma, H. A. "Grensverleggende Exploratie: Een(Godsdienst)Psychologische Verkenning van Verbeelding." *Nederlands Theologisch Tijdschrift* 56 (2002) 115–29.
Anderson, L. W., and D. R. Krathwohl, eds. *A Taxonomy for Learning, Teaching, and Assessing: A Revision of Bloom's Taxonomy of Educational Objectives.* Abridged ed. New York: Longman, 2001.
Avest, I. ter, and D. Clement. *Samen School Maken in de Bijlmer. Culturele Diversiteit en/in Schoolcultuur.* Amsterdam: Vrije Universiteit, 2008.
Avram, S., and J. Dronkers. "Religion and Schooling: The European Context." In *Worldview Education in a Multicultural Europe*, edited by E. Smith et al., 15–36. Basingstoke, UK: Palgrave MacMillan, 2013.
Bakker, C., ed. *Levensbeschouwelijk Onderwijs voor Alle Leerlingen.* Utrecht, Netherlands: Agilo, 2012.
Becker, J., and J. de Hart. *Godsdienstige Veranderingen in Nederland.* The Hague, Netherlands: SCP, 2006.
Berg, B. van den. *Speelruimte voor Dialoog en Verbeelding. Basisschoolleerlingen MakenKennis met Religieuze Verhalen. Een Narratief Ontwikkelingsgericht Onderzoek.* Gorinchem, Netherlands: Narratio, 2014.
Berg, B. van den, and A. Mulder, ed. *Leren van Betekenis. Dialogisch Levensbeschouwelijk Onderwijs op Negen Basisscholen.* Utrecht, Netherlands: Marnix Academie, 2017.
Berg, B. van den, et al. *Geloof Je het Zelf?! Levensbeschouwelijk Leren in het Primair Onderwijs.* Utrecht, Netherlands: Marnix Academie, 2013.
Bernts, T., and J. Berghuijs. *God in Nederland, 1966–2015.* Utrecht, Netherlands: Ten Have, 2016.
Biesta, G. *Good Education in an Age of Measurement: Ethics, Politics, Democracy.* Boulder, CO: Paradigm, 2010.
Brink, G. van den, ed. *De Lage Landen en het Hogere. De Betekenis van Geestelijke Beginselen in het Moderne Bestaan.* Amsterdam: Amsterdam University Press, 2012.

Bibliography

Bruner, J. S. *The Culture of Education*. Cambridge: Harvard University Press, 1996.

Castelijns, J., and B. van den Berg. *Een Leraar Blijf Je Altijd. Verhalen van Leraren over Persoonlijk Meesterschap*. Utrecht, Netherlands: CEPM, 2015.

CoE. *Recommendation 1720 Education and Religion*. Parliamentary Assembly debate, October 4, 2005 (27h Sitting).

———. *Religious Diversity and Intercultural Education: A Reference Book*. Edited by J. Keast. Provisional ed. 2006. Accessed April 26, 2017, http://tandis.odihr.pl/documents/hre-compendium/rus/CD%20SEC%202%20ENV/PR%20SEC%202/CoE%20Religious%20diversity%20ENG.pdf.

———. *Signposts: Policy and Practice for Teaching about Religions and Non-religious World Views in Intercultural Education*. Written by R. Jackson. Strasbourg: Council of Europe, 2014.

Derroitte, H., et al. "Worldview Education at Schools in Belgium." In *Worldview Education at Schools in Europe*, part 2, Western Europe, edited by M. Rothgangel et al., 43–64. Göttingen, Germany: V&R Unipress, 2014.

Dijkstra, A., et al., eds. *Verzuiling in het Onderwijs*. Groningen, Netherlands: Wolters Noordhoff, 1997.

Dillen, A. "Religious Participation of Children as Active Subjects: Toward a Hermeneutical-Communicative Model of Religious Education in Families with Young Children. *International Journal of Children's Spirituality* 12 (2007) 37–49. DOI: 10.1080/13644360701266119.

Egan, K. *The Educated Mind: How Cognitive Tools Shape Our Understanding*. Chicago: University of Chicago Press, 1997.

———. *An Imaginative Approach to Teaching*. San Francisco: Jossey-Bass, 2005.

Geurts, T., et al. "Religious Education in the Netherlands." In *Religious Education at Schools in Europe*, part 2, Western Europe, edited by M. Rothgangel et al., 171–204. Göttingen, Germany: V & R Unipress, 2014.

Harst, A. van der, et al. *Verhalen Verbinden. Ruimte voor Vertellen op de School*. Amersfoort, Netherlands: CPS, 2007.

Hart, J. de. *Zwevende Gelovigen*. The Hague, Netherlands: Sociaal Cultureel Planbureau, 2013.

Hermans, C. A. M. *Participerend Leren. Grondslagen van Religieuze Vorming in een Globaliserende Samenleving*. Budel, Netherlands: Damon, 2001.

Illeris, K. *How We Learn: Learning and Non-learning in School and Beyond*. London: Routledge, 2007.

Jackson, R. *Rethinking Religious Education and Plurality: Issues in Diversity and Pedagogy*. London: RoutledgeFalmer, 2004.

Kearney, R. *Poetics of Imagining: Modern to Post-modern*. New York: Fordham University Press, 1998.

Kelchtermans, G. *De Professionele Ontwikkeling van Leerkrachten Basisonderwijs vanuit Biografisch Perspectief*. Leuven, Belgium: Universitaire Pers Leuven, 1994.

Bibliography

———."Teachers' Emotions in Educational Reforms: Self-Understanding, Vulnerable Commitment and Micropolitical Literacy." *Teaching and Teacher Education* 21 (2005) 995–1006.

Kooij, J. van der. *Worldview and Moral Education: On Conceptual Clarity and Consistency in Use*. Amsterdam: GVO drukkers, 2016.

Letschert, J., et al., eds. *Beyond Storyline: Features, Principles and Pedagogical Profundity*. Enschede, Netherlands: SLO Curriculum Development Studies, 2006.

Lombaerts, H. "A Hermeneutical-Communicative Concept of Teaching Religion." *Journal of Religious Education* 48 (2000) 2–7.

Lomos, C., et al. "Professional Communities and Student Achievement—A Meta-analysis." *School Effectiveness and School Improvement* 22 (2011) 121–48.

Maex, J. *Een Hermeneutisch-Communicatief Concept Vakdidactiek Godsdienst: Een Fundamenteel-Theoretisch Empirisch Onderzoek*. PhD diss., Catholic University of Louvain, 2003.

Mette, N. "The Emergence of Hermeneutics in Catholic Religious Pedagogy and the Consequences of This Development: A Review of H. Halbfas' Book Fundamentalkatechetik (1968)." In *Hermeneutics and Worldview Education*, edited by H. Lombaerts and D. Pollefeyt, 57–72. Leuven, Belgium: Leuven University Press, 2004.

Moyaert, M. *Fragile Identities: Towards a Theology of Interreligious Hospitality*. Amsterdam: Rodopi, 2011.

Mulder, A. "Werken met Diepgang. Een Introductie." In *Werken met Diepgang. Levensbeschouwelijke Communicatie in de Praktijk van Onderwijs, Zorg en Kerk*, edited by A. Mulder and H. Snoek, 15–45. Zoetermeer, Netherlands: Meinema, 2012.

Nussbaum, M. C. *Not for Profit: Why Democracy Needs the Humanities*. Princeton: Princeton University Press, 2010.

Oers, B. van. *Ontwikkelingsgericht Werken in de Bovenbouw van de Basisschool. Een Theoretische Verkenning met het Oog op de Praktijk*. Alkmaar, Netherlands: De Activiteit, 2009.

Onderwijsraad. *Artikel 23 Grondwet in Maatschappelijk Perspectief*. The Hague, Netherlands: Onderwijsraad, 2012.

———. *Samen Leren Leven*. The Hague, Netherlands: Artoos, 2002.

OSCE/ODIHR. *Toledo Guiding Principles on Teaching about Religions and Beliefs in Public Schools*. Warsaw: Sungraf, 2007. Accessed April 26, 2017, https://www.osce.org/odihr/29154?download=true.

Parlevliet, L. J., et al. *Het Kind en de Grote Verhalen. Levensbeschouwelijk Leren in het Basisonderwijs*. Amersfoort, Netherlands: Kwintessens, 2013.

Platform Onderwijs 2032. *Ons onderwijs2032. Eindadvies*. The Hague, Netherlands: Bureau Platform Onderwijs2032, 2016.

Pollefeyt, D. "Difference Matters: A Hermeneutic-Communicative Concept of Didactics of Religion in a European Multi-religious Context." *Journal of Worldview Education* 56 (2008) 9–17.

Bibliography

———. "The Difference of Alterity: A Religious Pedagogy for an Interreligious and Interideological World." In *Responsibility, God and Society: Theological Ethics in Dialogue*, edited by J. de Tavenier et al., 305–30. Leuven, Belgium: Peeters, 2008.

———. *Reader: Course Didactics* (A0950), *Religious Education*, 2011. Accessed April 26, 2017, http://www.kuleuven.be/thomas/uploads/image/prvftp/A0950Reader.pdf.

Roebben, B. *Inclusieve Godsdienstpedagogiek. Grondlijnen voor Levensbeschouwelijke Vorming*. Leuven, Belgium: Acco, 2015.

Rothgangel, M., and H.-G. Ziebertz. "Worldview Education at Schools in Germany." With P. Klutz. In *Worldview Education at Schools in Europe*, part 1, *Central Europe*, edited by M. Rothgangel et al., 115–48. Göttingen, Germany: V&R Unipress, 2016.

Ruijters, M. *Liefde voor Leren. Over Diversiteit van Leren en Ontwikkelen in en van Organisaties*. Deventer, Germany: Kluwer, 2006.

Ruijters M., and R. J. Simons, ed. *Canon van het Leren. 50 Concepten en Hun Grondleggers*. Deventer, Germany: Kluwer, 2012.

Schepper, J. de. *Levensbeschouwing Ontwikkelen. Didactiek voor Levensbeschouwing in het Primair Onderwijs*. Amersfoort, Netherlands: Kwintessens, 2015.

Schaap, J. G. *Pedagogiek van Zingeving. Kennisbasis van Interactief Leren*. Leuven, Belgium: Garant, 2001.

Schweitzer, F. "The Hermeneutic Condition of Worldview Education." In *Hermeneutics and Worldview Education*, edited by H. Lombaerts and D. Pollefeyt, 73–88. Leuven, Belgium: Leuven University Press, 2004.

Smart, N. *The World's Religions*. Cambridge: Cambridge University Press, 1998.

Smith, E., et al. Introduction to *Worldview Education in a Multicultural Europe*, edited by E. Smith et al., 1–14. Basingstoke, UK: Palgrave MacMillan, 2013.

Stern, L. J. *The Spirit of the School*. London: Continuum, 2009.

www.ingramcontent.com/pod-product-compliance
Lightning Source LLC
Chambersburg PA
CBHW051109160426
43193CB00010B/1376